The Lord Jesus Christ: Fully Man and Fully God

EVIDENCE FROM THE BIBLE

By

Dr. Margaret Lepke and June Young

Biblical Publications

Biblical Publications

Email: biblicalpublications@gmail.com
Web: http://www.biblicalpublications.org

© Margaret Lepke & June Young 2017

All rights reserved. No part of this publication may be reproduced, stored in a retrieval system or transmitted, in any form, or by any means, electronic, mechanical, photocopying, recording or otherwise, without the prior permission of the publishers.

ISBN 978-0-6480443-1-4

Published 30 November, 2017 (2nd Edition)

Bible Verses:
Greek-English translation of John 1:1 on p.57 courtesy of http://biblehub.com/interlinear/john/1-1.htm
Unless otherwise indicated, Scripture quotations are from the New King James Version of the Holy Bible. Copyright 1983 by Thomas Nelson, Inc. Used by permission. All rights reserved.

Images:
P.26 Heart shaped line free vector; author: BSGStudio; free for commercial use with attribution; from all-free-lownload.com
P.62 Crown; free keep calm crown clipart; author: Josephine Alvarez, from clipartfest.com
P. 65 Resources image © Can Stock Photo / JohanH

DEDICATION

To Him who is able to keep you from stumbling
and to present you faultless
before the presence of His glory with exceeding joy.
To God our Savior, who alone is wise,
be glory and majesty,
dominion and power, both now and forever.
Amen.

Jude 1:24-25 NKJV

CONTENTS

The Lord Jesus Christ: Fully Man	7
Part 1 **The Lord Jesus Christ: Fully Man**	9
Part 2 **The Lord Jesus Christ: Two Natures**	15
• Who Was Jesus BEFORE His Earthly Life?	16
• Who Was Jesus DURING His Earthly Life?	20
• Who Is Jesus AFTER His Ascension to Heaven?	24
Part 3 **The Lord Jesus Christ: Fully God**	27
• Titles of Jesus	32
• Old Testament References	39
• New Testament References	43
⇾ Introduction to the Gospels	43
⇾ Synoptic Gospels	44
⇾ Gospel of John	45
⇾ Statements by Paul	52
⇾ Statements by Peter	58
⇾ Hebrews	59
⇾ Revelation	60
Final Words from the Authors	63

RESOURCES:

Answers to the John 1:1 Debate (Full Article)	66
Answers to the Trinity Debate (Free Download Info)	73
Jesus is coming back! (Free Eternity eBook Info)	74
Margaret's Testimony	75
Your Way to Eternal Life	79

Acknowledgements

We wish to thank Henry Lepke for his valuable contributions and steadfast support.

We also thank Rita Galieh, Patricia Scribner and Robert James for proof reading our manuscript and giving us comprehensive feedback. Additionally, we thank everyone who read the final draft and simply said, "Great! I want some of those when they are ready." We were very encouraged by your enthusiastic response.

Finally, we wish to express special gratitude to Dr. John Ecob and Dr. Gene Jeffries for their endorsements on the back cover, and to Barbara Stuart and Cynthia White for their emails and reader comments.

This is an important topic, and every one of you has helped to make this book what it is today. We pray that our Lord may richly reward you

A Note from the Authors

June and I (Margaret) met several years ago and soon discovered that we shared the same passion for God and his Word, the Bible. Whenever difficult topics arose, we would independently search for answers and pool our resources.

How this book came about... One day, the discussion in our Bible Study group focused on whether Jesus was truly God. Both June and I had previously spoken with people who didn't believe so, or weren't sure, and both of us had been on personal quests to settle this question for ourselves. So when the topic resurfaced, we searched for a book that would present a biblical view, was focused on Scripture rather than lengthy theological debates, and was reader-friendly yet comprehensive and concise. A book we could hand to someone who was seeking answers. When we couldn't find anything suitable, we decided to write the book we wanted to buy (that was my task).

Our qualifications... June has been studying the Bible since she became a Christian in 1980 and has always searched for answers that are consistent with everything the Bible has to say on a particular topic. She makes handwritten notes in her many journals and has a special interest in biblical prophecies concerning the Lord Jesus Christ. I (Margaret) became a Christian in 1983. Since then I have done much topical research, and my professional background includes Christian Counselling, Adult Education, Theology, and a PhD in Biblical Studies. If you are interested, you can read my testimony on page 75. Considering our backgrounds, pooling resources and writing this book was the logical thing to do.

Our aim is to help you know the Lord Jesus more intimately by taking you on a journey through the Bible. You will read many exciting things about him and experience God's Word speaking straight to your heart (we have printed all verses in full). Whether you want to learn more yourself or need a suitable resource to share with others, this little book will be of great value.

Bible quotes are taken from the NKJV because we prefer a direct translation rather than a more subjective, meaning-based one, and all verses are printed in italics for easy distinction. Please note that pronouns referring to deity are capitalised in the NKJV, and Scripture portions referring to Old Testament prophecies are printed in upper-case. These distinctives have been retained in all Bible quotations. Furthermore, the American spelling of 'savior' in these quotes has been retained throughout the text of this book to avoid stumbling over what may otherwise be considered mistakes (in Australia we spell the word 'saviour').

We hope that as you read, you will develop a glorious vision of the Lord Jesus Christ and be inspired to love and serve him with all your heart. We have a living savior!

Margaret Lepke & June Young

Part 1
The Lord Jesus Christ: Fully Man

A good place to start is always at the beginning. Most people believe that Jesus existed as a man. The Bible confirms it, and secular historians agree. Jesus claimed to be someone important, and he was. Has any other man ever had the honour of referencing time? Since the Gregorian calendar was adopted as the civil calendar of the West, time has been divided into B.C. = Before Christ, and A.D. = Anno Domini, in the year of our Lord. What a tribute to the man Jesus Christ! But human acclaim is not enough. To discover his true identity, we need to find out what God's Word, the Bible, has to say about him.

First, let us examine his humanity. Did you know that the Bible records **seven important facts** to confirm that Jesus was truly human? Let's find out what they are. All verses from the Bible are printed in italics.

1. Jesus had a human genealogy

His genealogy in Matthew traces the ancestry of Mary's husband Joseph as the son of King David. Have you ever noticed that Joseph is called 'the husband of Mary' instead of 'the father of Jesus?' I love the fact that God is so precise and wants us to notice these details often missed by the casual reader. This is what the Bible says,

> *"The book of the genealogy of Jesus Christ, the Son of David, the Son of Abraham: Abraham begot Isaac, Isaac begot Jacob, and Jacob begot Judah and his brothers ... And Jacob begot Joseph the husband of Mary, of whom was born Jesus who is called Christ."* (Matthew 1:1-16)

Luke's genealogy traces the ancestry of Jesus past King David right back to the very beginning, to Adam and God:

> *"Now Jesus Himself began His ministry at about thirty years of age, being (as was supposed) the son of Joseph, the son of Heli, ... the son of Enosh, the son of Seth, the son of Adam, the son of God."* (Luke 3:23-38)

Did you notice that this account differs from that in Matthew? Scholars believe that Luke's genealogy is traced through Mary, the daughter of Heli, which is entirely plausible because the general custom was to exclude women from the line of succession, hence Joseph would have been listed as the son, i.e. son-in-law, of Heli in Mary's place.

Even in his glorified post-resurrection state Jesus acknowledged his earthly genealogy as the offspring of King David when appearing to the apostle John:

> *"I, Jesus, have sent My angel to testify to you these things in the churches. I am the Root and the Offspring of David, the Bright and Morning Star."* (Revelation 22:16)

2. Jesus fully experienced humanity while on earth

He had a human birth:

> *"And Jacob begot Joseph the husband of Mary, of whom was born Jesus who is called Christ."* (Matthew 1:16)

> *"Now after Jesus was born in Bethlehem of Judea in the days of Herod the king, behold, wise men from the East came to Jerusalem, saying, "Where is He who has been born King of the Jews? For we have seen His star in the East and have come to worship Him."* (Matthew 2:1-2)

He was circumcised:

> *"And when eight days were completed for the circumcision of the Child, His name was called JESUS, the name given by the angel before He was conceived in the womb."* (Luke 2:21) [The name 'Jesus' means 'rescuer, deliverer, savior' –he saves his people from their sins.]

He ate food:

"And the Pharisees and scribes complained, saying, "This Man receives sinners and eats with them." (Luke 15:2)

He wept:

"Now as He drew near, He saw the city and wept over it…" (Luke 19:41)

"Jesus wept [after Lazarus had died]." (John 11:35)

He was weary:

"Now Jacob's well was there. Jesus therefore, being wearied from His journey, sat thus by the well. It was about the sixth hour." (John 4:6)

He slept:

"And suddenly a great tempest arose on the sea, so that the boat was covered with the waves. But He [Jesus] was asleep." (Matthew 8:24)

He was tempted:

"For we do not have a High Priest who cannot sympathize with our weaknesses, but was in all points tempted as we are, yet without sin." (Hebrews 4:15)

He suffered:

"For to this you were called, because Christ also <u>suffered</u> for us, leaving us an example, that you should follow His steps: "WHO COMMITTED NO SIN, NOR WAS DECEIT FOUND IN HIS MOUTH"; who, when He was reviled, did not revile in return; when He <u>suffered</u>, He did not threaten, but committed Himself to Him who judges righteously; who Himself <u>bore our sins</u> in His own body on the tree, that we, having died to sins, might live for righteousness—by whose stripes you were healed." (1 Peter 2:21-24)

He died:
> "But one of the soldiers pierced His side with a spear, and immediately blood and water came out." (John 19:34)

> "God demonstrates His own love toward us, in that while we were still sinners, Christ died for us." (Romans 5:8)

He had a body of flesh and blood:
> "For many deceivers have gone out into the world who do not confess Jesus Christ as coming in the flesh. This is a deceiver and an antichrist." (2 John 1:7)

3. He retained the body of a man following his resurrection

> "Behold My hands and My feet, that it is I Myself. Handle Me and see, for a spirit does not have flesh and bones as you see I have." When He had said this, He showed them His hands and His feet. But while they still did not believe for joy, and marveled, He said to them, "Have you any food here?" So they gave Him a piece of a broiled fish and some honeycomb. And He took it and ate in their presence." (Luke 24:39-43)

> "Him God raised up on the third day, and showed Him openly, not to all the people, but to witnesses chosen before by God, even to us who ate and drank with Him after He arose from the dead." (Acts 10:40-41)

4. He retained the body of a man following his ascension

> "But he [talking about Stephen], being full of the Holy Spirit, gazed into heaven and saw the glory of God, and Jesus standing at the right hand of God, and said, "Look! I see the heavens opened and the Son of Man standing at the right hand of God!" (Acts 7:55)

5. He is referred to as a man in his role as mediator

> "For there is one God and one Mediator between God and men, the Man Christ Jesus, who gave Himself a ransom for all, to be testified in due time." (1 Timothy 2:5-6)

6. He is referred to as a man in his role as judge of the world

"Truly, these times of ignorance God overlooked, but now commands all men everywhere to repent, because He has appointed a day on which He will judge the world in righteousness by the Man whom He has ordained. He has given assurance of this to all by raising Him from the dead." (Acts 17:30-31)

"For as the Father has life in Himself, so He has granted the Son to have life in Himself, and has given Him authority to execute judgment also, because He is the Son of Man." (John 5:26-27)

7. When he returns to the earth, Jesus will return as a man

"His feet will stand in that day on the Mount of Olives, which is before Jerusalem on the east; and the Mount of Olives will be split in two, from east to west, making a very great valley. Half of the mountain will move toward the north, and half of it toward the south." (Zechariah 14:4)

"While they were looking steadfastly into the sky as he went, behold, two men stood by them in white clothing, who also said, "You men of Galilee, why do you stand looking into the sky? This Jesus, who was received up from you into the sky, will come back in the same way as you saw him going into the sky." (Acts 1:10-11)

~~~

Time is short – Jesus is coming again!
If you are interested in finding out more about his coming again, you can download a free eBook titled *Eternity to Eternity*. It explains Christ's return in the overall context of God's plan for the ages (see download info on page 74).

The Greatest Man in history is Jesus.
He had no servants, yet they called Him Master.
He had no degree, yet they called Him Teacher.
He had no medicines, yet they called Him Healer.
He had no army, yet kings feared Him.
He won no military battles, yet He conquered the world.
He committed no crime, yet they crucified Him.
He was buried in a tomb, yet He lives today.

WITH GRATITUDE TO THE UNKNOWN AUTHOR

Part 2
The Lord Jesus Christ: Two Natures

*"If he be not God, he could not be the Almighty Savior.
If he be not man, he could not indeed have died at all."*
ANON

The big question is, "Was Jesus nothing more than a human being?" If so, his death would have been nothing more than a sad ending to life, and his blood would have had no efficacy to atone for man's (mankind's) sins. No mere man is able to atone for sins. Only a perfect, sinless sacrifice is fit for this task, and according to the Bible no human being is without sin:

> *"As it is written, "There is no one righteous; no, not one ... for all have sinned, and fall short of the glory of God."* (Romans 3:10,23)

However, the Bible assures us that Christ WAS that acceptable, blameless, perfect sacrifice sent by God:

> *"But God demonstrates His own love toward us, in that while we were still sinners, Christ died for us. Much more then, having now been justified by His blood, we shall be saved from wrath through Him. For if when we were enemies we were reconciled to God through the death of His Son, much more, having been reconciled, we shall be saved by His life. And not only that, but we also rejoice in God through our Lord Jesus Christ, through whom we have now received the reconciliation."* (Romans 5:8-11)

So how could Jesus be a man and a sinless sacrifice at the same time? The Bible says that he knew no sin:

"For him [Jesus] *who knew no sin he* [God] *made to be sin on our behalf; so that in him we might become the righteousness of God"* (2 Corinthians 5:21).

What happened to make this possible?

In order to understand who Jesus really is, and why his death can bring us life, we need to grasp that he was not JUST a man while on earth (or an angel, as some have claimed, or half man and half God), but that in him – in the one person – were combined two separate, yet complete, natures. He was fully God and fully man.

This union of two natures is more easily comprehended if we first understand the identity of Jesus during different time periods:

- BEFORE he began his earthly life,
- DURING his earthly life, and
- AFTER his ascension.

Let's begin with his pre-existence...

▪ Who Was Jesus BEFORE His Earthly Life?

Before his earthly life, Jesus was the Spiritual Rock

The apostle Paul tells us that it was Jesus who followed the Israelites as a 'spiritual rock' during their time in the wilderness:

"And all drank the same spiritual drink. For they drank of that spiritual Rock that followed them, and that Rock was Christ." (1 Corinthians 10:4)

He was also the Angel of the LORD

In the Old Testament, Jesus appeared numerous times in human form as a Christophany, an Old Testament appearance of Christ before his human birth. In this particular form of appearance, he was called 'the Angel of the LORD.' Dr. John Walvoord, president of Dallas Theological Seminary from 1952 to 1986, taught that "It is safe to assume that every visible manifestation of God in bodily form in the Old Testament is to be identified with the Lord Jesus Christ." (www.christology101.com)

Because 'The Angel of the LORD' is one of his titles, some people argue that Jesus was an actual angel. This is not true! Whilst it is true that the Hebrew word 'malak' (translated 'angel') simply means 'messenger' and can refer to either human, angelic or divine beings, this special 'Messenger of the LORD' was definitely divine. When he appeared to Sarah's maid Hagar, his divinity was made very obvious (see next verse).

As the Angel of the LORD, Jesus appeared to Hagar:

> *"Now the <u>Angel of the LORD</u> found her [Hagar] by a spring of water in the wilderness, by the spring on the way to Shur. And He said, "Hagar, Sarai's maid, where have you come from, and where are you going?" She said, "I am fleeing from the presence of my mistress Sarai." The Angel of the LORD said to her, "Return to your mistress, and submit yourself under her hand." Then the Angel of the LORD said to her, "<u>I will multiply your descendants</u> exceedingly, so that they shall not be counted for multitude." And the Angel of the LORD said to her: "Behold, you are with child, and you shall bear a son. You shall call his name Ishmael, because the LORD has heard your affliction. He shall be a wild man; his hand shall be against every man, and every man's hand against him. And he shall dwell in the presence of all his brethren." Then she called the name of <u>the LORD who spoke to her</u>, <u>You-Are-the-God-Who-Sees</u>; for she said, "Have I also here seen Him who sees me?" Therefore the well was called Beer Lahai Roi; observe, it is between Kadesh and Bered."* (Genesis 16:7-14)

This messenger had the power to multiply Hagar's descendants, which means he could not have been an angelic being. Hagar recognised him as God and named him, "<u>You-Are-the-God-Who-Sees</u>."

The Bible repeatedly tells us that the LORD (Yahweh/Jehovah) cannot be seen by human eyes. For instance, the LORD said to Moses,

"You cannot see My face; for no man shall see Me, and live." (Exodus 33:20)

But there is someone who is the very image of the LORD, who has declared him. He can be seen. His name is Jesus. People saw him as a Christophany in the Old Testament and as the man Jesus Christ during his life on earth.

"No one has seen God at any time. The only begotten Son, who is in the bosom of the Father, He has declared Him." (John 1:18)

"He [Jesus] is the image of the invisible God." (Colossians 1:15)

We should therefore not be surprised to learn that this 'Messenger of the LORD' in the Old Testament was Jesus, who said of himself, *"Most assuredly, I say to you, before Abraham was, I AM."* (John 8:58)

Jesus laid claim to deity by saying,

"I am the Alpha and the Omega, the Beginning and the End, the First and the Last." (Revelation 22:13).

As the Angel of the LORD, Jesus also appeared to Abraham:

"But the Angel of the LORD called to him [Abraham] from heaven and said, "Abraham, Abraham!" So he said, "Here I am." Then the <u>Angel of the LORD</u> called to Abraham a second time out of heaven, and said: "By Myself I have sworn, says the <u>LORD</u>, because you have done this thing, and have not withheld your son, your only son — blessing I will bless you, and multiplying I will multiply your descendants as the stars of the heaven and as the sand which is on the seashore; and your descendants shall possess the gate of their enemies." (Genesis 22:11; 15-17)

Did you notice that the Angel of the LORD swore by himself to multiply Abraham's descendants? Only God can do that.

And finally, as the Angel of the LORD, Jesus appeared to Moses:

> *And the <u>Angel of the LORD</u> appeared to him* [Moses] *in a flame of fire from the midst of a bush. So he looked, and behold, the bush was burning with fire, but the bush was not consumed. Then Moses said, "I will now turn aside and see this great sight, why the bush does not burn." So when the <u>LORD</u> saw that he turned aside to look, <u>God</u> called to him from the midst of the bush and said, "Moses, Moses!" And he said, "Here I am."* (Exodus 3:2-4)

In this passage, 'The Angel of the LORD,' 'LORD' and 'God' are used interchangeably!

He was the Angel of His Presence

In Isaiah we read that the LORD became Israel's savior, and that 'the Angel of His Presence' saved the people. Isaiah speaks of YHWH (Yahweh/ Jehovah) as the redeemer of his people while the New Testament reveals that it is Jesus who is the redeemer. YHWH and Jesus are therefore equal in their power to redeem, and 'the Angel of His Presence' in the following passage is another Christophany.

> Isaiah said, *"I will mention the lovingkindnesses of the LORD and the praises of the LORD, according to all that the LORD has bestowed on us, and the great goodness toward the house of Israel, which He has bestowed on them according to His mercies, according to the multitude of His lovingkindnesses. for He said, "Surely they are My people, Children who will not lie." So <u>He</u>* [the LORD] *<u>became their Savior</u>. In all their affliction He was afflicted, and <u>the Angel of His Presence saved them</u>; In His love and in His pity He redeemed them; and He bore them and carried them all the days of old. But they rebelled and grieved His Holy Spirit; so He turned Himself against them as an enemy, and He fought against them."* (Isaiah 63:7-10)

He was the Great Creator

> *For by Him* [Jesus] *all things were created that are in heaven and that are on earth, visible and invisible, whether thrones or dominions or*

principalities or powers. All things were created through Him and for Him. (Colossians 1:16)

And finally, he was the Word

In the beginning was the Word, and the Word was with God, and <u>the Word was God</u>. (John 1:1)

The Word became flesh and lived among us. We saw his glory, such glory as of the one and only Son of the Father, full of grace and truth. (John 1:14)

Dear Reader,

If you are a Jehovah's Witness and have been taught that this translation of John 1:1 is incorrect, please do not stop reading at this point! We have included a special section for you where we present both biblical and grammatical evidence for a correct translation of this verse. You will find this information in the resources section on page 66, titled *Answers to the John 1:1 Debate*.

- **Who Was Jesus DURING His Earthly Life?**

During his earthly life, Jesus was God in flesh

When the "Word" became flesh and received the name 'Jesus,' he fully retained his God nature while taking on humanity:

"Let this mind be in you, which was also in Christ Jesus: Who, <u>being in the form</u> [nature] <u>of God</u>, thought it<u> not robbery to be equal with God</u> but made himself of no reputation, <u>taking the form of a bondservant, and coming in the likeness of men</u>. And being found in appearance as a man, He humbled Himself and became obedient to the point of death, even the death of the cross. (Philippians 2:5-8)

In other words, God became flesh to come to earth as a man. Jesus was equal with God while at the same time humbling himself as a man. Therefore he was called 'Son of Man' and also 'Son of God,' combining two natures in his earthly body. In case you wish to read more on this topic elsewhere, the theological term for this phenomenon is 'hypostatic union.'

He shared God's glory before the world was made

"And now, O Father, glorify Me together with Yourself, with the glory which I had with You before the world was." (John 17:5)

His true residence was in heaven from where he came

"No one has ascended to heaven but He who came down from heaven, that is, the Son of Man who is in heaven." (John 3:13)

He knew all things and had all power

"Jesus saw Nathanael coming toward Him, and said of him, "Behold, an Israelite indeed, in whom is no deceit!" Nathanael said to Him, "How do You know me?" Jesus answered and said to him, "Before Philip called you, when you were under the fig tree, I saw you." Nathanael answered and said to Him, "Rabbi, You are the Son of God! You are the King of Israel!" Jesus answered and said to him, "Because I said to you, 'I saw you under the fig tree,' do you believe? You will see greater things than these." (John 1:47-50)

"But Jesus did not commit Himself to them, because He knew all men [people]*, and had no need that anyone should testify of man, for He knew what was in man."* (John 2:24-25)

"…and [he] *rebuked the winds and the sea, and there was a great calm."* (Matthew 8:26)

He walked on water (Matt.14:26-27), fed the multitudes (Matt.14:15-21), and raised Lazarus who had been dead four days. (John 11:32-45)

Before returning to heaven, Jesus said, *"I am with you always, even to the end of the age."* (Matthew 28:20)

He was without sin

As the Son of Man, Jesus came 'in the likeness of men' because he took on a human body without sharing in its sin nature. He was WITHOUT SIN. Unlike all other human beings, Jesus never sinned, not even once.

Of the human race, the Bible says,

> *"As it is written: "THERE IS NONE RIGHTEOUS, NO, NOT ONE ... for all have sinned and fall short of the glory of God."* (Romans 3:10, 23)

But of Jesus, the Bible says:

> *"WHO COMMITTED NO SIN, NOR WAS DECEIT FOUND IN HIS MOUTH"* (1 Peter 2:22)
>
> *"And you know that He was manifested to take away our sins, and in Him there is no sin."* (1 John 3:5)
>
> *"[God] made Him [Jesus] who knew no sin to be sin for us, that we might become the righteousness of God in Him."* (2 Corinthians 5:21)
>
> *"For we do not have a High Priest who cannot sympathize with our weaknesses, but was in all points tempted as we are, yet without sin."* (Hebrews 4:15)

The apostle Paul warned us about false teachers who would deny that God came in the flesh:

> *"Beware lest anyone cheat you through philosophy and empty deceit, according to the tradition of men, according to the basic principles of the world, and not according to Christ. For <u>in Him dwells all the fullness of the Godhead bodily</u>; and you* [a born-again Christian] *are complete in Him, who is the head of all principality and power."* (Colossians 2:8-10)

Being without sin, he was able to forgive sins

> *"When Jesus saw their faith, He said to the paralytic, "Son, your sins are forgiven you." And some of the scribes were sitting there and*

reasoning in their hearts, "Why does this Man speak blasphemies like this? Who can forgive sins but God alone?" (Mark 2:5-7)

Because the fullness of the Godhead dwelt in the human body of Jesus, he spoke truthfully when he claimed to be one with the Father. The following table provides a few examples of both human and divine natures operating during the earthly life of Jesus.

TABLE OF HUMAN AND DIVINE NATURES IN OPERATION

Humanity	JESUS	Divinity
He had a body of flesh and bones (Luke 24:39)	And yet…	The fullness of deity dwelt in him (Col. 2:9)
He had to grow in wisdom (Luke 2:52)	And yet…	He knew all things (John 21:17)
He was tempted (Matthew 4:1)	And yet…	He was sinless (1 Peter 2:22; Hebr.4:15)
He prayed to the Father (John 17)	And yet…	He responded to prayer (John 14:14)
He worshiped the Father (John 17)	And yet…	He was worshiped by men (Matt. 2:2, 11; 14:33)
He was called 'man' (Mark 15:39; John 19:5)	And yet…	He was called 'God' (John 20:28; Hebrews 1:8)
He was called Son of Man (John 9:35-37)	And yet…	He was called Son of God (Mark 1:1; 15:39)
He died (Romans 5:8)	And yet…	He was able to give eternal life (John 10:28)

▪ Who Is Jesus AFTER His Ascension to Heaven?

When Jesus came to earth as a man, he fully retained his God nature. In like manner, when he returned to heaven from where he had come, he also retained his perfect human nature (which had remained sinless while on earth). Even as the risen Christ, Jesus still referred to his earthly address in the present tense when he spoke to the apostle Paul. This is Paul's account:

> *"And I fell to the ground and heard a voice saying to me, 'Saul, Saul, why are you persecuting Me?' So I answered, 'Who are You, Lord?' And He said to me, 'I am Jesus of Nazareth, whom you are persecuting.'"* (Acts 22:7-8)

At the same time Jesus also referred to himself as God when he spoke to the apostle John:

> *"I am the Alpha and the Omega, the Beginning and the End,"* says the Lord, *"who is and who was and who is to come, the Almighty."* (Revelation 1:8)

Following his ascension, Jesus took on three roles that require a perfect human nature (yet without sin) and a perfect God nature:

Jesus – the Redeemer

> *"For the grace of God that brings salvation has appeared to all men, teaching us that, denying ungodliness and worldly lusts, we should live soberly, righteously, and godly in the present age, looking for the blessed hope and glorious appearing of our great God and Savior Jesus Christ, who gave Himself for us, that He might redeem us from every lawless deed and purify for Himself His own special people, zealous for good works."* (Titus 2:11-14)

Jesus – the Mediator

> *"For there is one God and one Mediator between God and men, the Man Christ Jesus."* (1 Timothy 2:5)

Jesus – the Righteous Judge

The Old Testament declares that it is the LORD (Yahweh/Jehovah) who will be the judge of the earth:

> *"For He* [the LORD] *is coming to judge the earth. With righteousness He shall judge the world, and the peoples with equity."* (Psalm 98:8-9)

But the New Testament explains that it will be the Son of God, Jesus, who will judge the world. When Paul spoke to the Athenians, he said:

> *"*[God] *now commands all men everywhere to repent, because He has appointed a day on which He will judge the world in righteousness by the Man whom He has ordained* [Paul is speaking of Jesus, the Son of God]. *He has given assurance of this to all by raising Him from the dead."* (Acts 17:30-31)

The Lord Jesus Christ will judge the whole world!

To summarise our discussion of Christ's two natures, we may confidently say that God, the Word, came to earth as the Son of Man. Retaining his God nature while adding a sinless human nature, he was born both Son of Man and Son of God.

As Charles A. Clough puts it:

"The virgin conception made possible the incarnation of Jesus Christ, Who at once was both Creator and creature. He was then and remains both undiminished deity and true humanity, the two natures being inseparably united in one Person, without mixture, transfer, or confusion of any attributes, the union being personal and eternal." (Quoted from *A Biblical Framework for Worship and Obedience in an Age of Global Deception: an Introduction*) The Bible Framework is a six part study course with 224 audio lessons and notes, designed to root your thinking in the framework of truth found throughout the Bible. Free downloads are available from www.BibleFramework.com.

The dual nature of our Lord Jesus Christ is the reason why he was the only perfect human being who ever lived. Remaining without sin throughout his life, he was then qualified to pay the price for the sins of the whole world by shedding his innocent blood. That is why the apostle Paul was able to say,

> "I declare to you the gospel [good news] ... that Christ died for our sins according to the Scriptures, and that He was buried, and that He rose again the third day according to the Scriptures, and that He was seen by Cephas [Peter], then by the twelve. After that He was seen by over five hundred brethren at once, of whom the greater part remain to the present, but some have fallen asleep. After that He was seen by James, then by all the apostles. Then last of all He was seen by me also..." (1 Corinthians 15:1-8)

The Son of God became the savior of the world. He died, he rose again, he returned to heaven. What a marvellous God we have!

*"For God so loved the world
that He gave His only begotten Son,
that whoever believes in Him
should not perish but have everlasting life."*

(John 3:16)

Part 3
The Lord Jesus Christ: Fully God

> *The natural mind cannot understand it,*
> *The spiritual mind cannot fully comprehend it,*
> *The scriptures of God reveal it,*
> *And therefore we believe it!*
> ANON

First, we need to say a few words about the doctrine of the Trinity, although we are not going to discuss it in detail. You may already know that the word itself is not found in the Bible, but we cannot get away from the fact that many Bible passages clearly show that God is one in plurality and, more specifically, three in one. If you have been an avid opponent of the Trinitarian concept, please don't stop reading at this point. Ponder the following verses and the rest of this chapter, and ask God to show you the truth. If you would like to read more about the subject, you can download a short eBook named 'Answers to the Trinity Debate' from biblicalpublications.org/ebooks.html. More info on p.73.

God is one in plurality

No one can reasonably deny that the God of the Bible is one God in plurality. It is cemented even in the famous Deuteronomic Creed (although most non-Messianic Jews would probably not want to acknowledge this):

> *"Hear, O Israel: The LORD our God, the LORD is one!"*
> (Deuteronomy 6: 4)

The expanded translation puts the word 'one' into context by explaining that it means 'properly united':

> "Hear, O Israel, Yahweh/Jehovah our Elohim [plural] is one [properly united] Yahweh/Jehovah."

Equally correct translation:

> "Yahweh/Jehovah our Elohim is a united Yahweh/Jehovah."

The word 'one' in Deuteronomy 6:4 refers to something that is a unity, not a single entity. The same word is used in Genesis 2:24 to speak of the one-ness of husband and wife (two as one).

> *"Therefore a man shall leave his father and mother and be joined to his wife, and they shall become one flesh."* (Genesis 2:24)

The very first sentence of Scripture refers to this concept by using the plural, masculine noun Elohim when referring to the creator of the universe, but then following this plural noun with a singular verb form:

> *"In the beginning, God* [Elohim, plural] *created* [bara, singular] *the heavens and the earth."* (Genesis 1:1)

And that is not all. The concept of God as one in plurality is purposely repeated in Genesis 1:26 where God says,

> *"Let us make man in our image, after our likeness."* (Genesis 1:26)

The grammatical structure clearly indicates that God spoke to someone else who co-created with him.

Who was that someone else? Did God speak to angels? The answer is clearly no because Nehemiah addressed God alone when he said,

> *"You alone are the LORD; You have made heaven, the heaven of heavens, with all their host, the earth and everything on it, the seas and all that is in them, and You preserve them all. The host of heaven worships You."* (Nehemiah 9:6)

In other words, the host of heaven, the angelic beings, worship God but were not involved in the act of creation. Job confirmed this when he said,

> *"The morning stars sang together and all the sons of God* [here referring to angels] *shouted for joy when God created the earth."* (Job 38:7)

Since the angels were clearly not involved, who did God address as co-creator? As we will see in a moment, it was Jesus!

Genesis tells us that God spoke all things into being and that the Holy Spirit was present during creation:

> *"The earth was without form, and void; and darkness was on the face of the deep. And the <u>Spirit of God</u> was hovering over the face of the waters."*
> (Genesis 1:2)

> *"Then <u>God</u> [Elohim] <u>said</u>, "Let there be light"; and there was light."*
> (Genesis 1:3)

But then the New Testament more clearly reveals that it was Jesus (as the Word of God) through whom and by whom all things were created:

> *"In the beginning was the Word, and the Word was with God, and the Word was God. He was in the beginning with God. All things were made through Him, and without Him nothing was made that was made. "* (John 1:1-3)

> *"He was in the world, and the world was made through Him, and the world did not know Him … And the Word became flesh and dwelt among us, and we beheld His glory, the glory as of the only begotten of the Father, full of grace and truth."* (John 1:10, 14) Note: these verses are talking about Jesus.

> *For by Him* [Jesus] *all things were created that are in heaven and that are on earth, visible and invisible, whether thrones or dominions or principalities or powers. All things were created through Him and for*

> Him. And He is before all things, and in Him all things consist...
> (Colossians 1:16-17)

Not only is Jesus the great creator, he is also the very image of God and the only one who has ever declared God to mankind:

> *"The god of this world* [Satan/the devil] *hath blinded the minds of them which believe not, lest the light of the glorious gospel of Christ, who is the image of God, should shine unto them."* (2 Corinthians 4:4)

> *"No one has seen God at any time. The only begotten Son, who is in the bosom of the Father, He has declared Him."* (John 1:18)

Following are a few more New Testament verses that support this one-ness in plurality regarding the Father, the Son, and the Holy Spirit:

Both Father and Son (Jesus) send the Spirit

> *"But the Helper, the Holy Spirit, whom the <u>Father will send in My name</u>, He will teach you all things, and bring to your remembrance all things that I said to you.* (John 14:26)

> *"Nevertheless I tell you the truth. It is to your advantage that I go away; for if I do not go away, the Helper will not come to you; but if I depart, <u>I will send Him to you</u>."* (John 16:7)

Jesus owns all things belonging to the Father

> Jesus said, *"However, when He, the Spirit of truth, has come, He will guide you into all truth; for He will not speak on His own authority, but whatever He hears He will speak; and He will tell you things to come. <u>He will glorify Me</u>, for He will take of what is Mine and declare it to you. <u>All things that the Father has are Mine</u>. Therefore I said that He will take of Mine and declare it to you."* (John 16:13-15)

Father, Son and Holy Spirit – these three are one

> *"For there are three that bear witness in heaven: the Father, the Word, and the Holy Spirit; and these three are one."* (1 John 5:7)

"Go therefore and make disciples of all the nations, baptizing them in the <u>name</u> [singular] of <u>the Father and of the Son and of the Holy Spirit</u> [plurality], teaching them to observe all things that I have commanded you; and lo, I am with you always, even to the end of the age." "Amen." (Matthew 28:19-20)

"The grace of the Lord Jesus Christ, and the love of God, and the communion of the Holy Spirit be with you all. Amen." (2 Corinthians 13:14)

Our resource on page 73 refers to more teaching on this concept of God being one in plurality. It provides download details for a free, short eBook named *Answers to the Trinity Debate* which explains the Trinity in a nutshell.

Now let us return to the deity of Jesus. There are many scriptures in both Old and New Testaments that confirm this truth. Our aim is to present sufficient evidence without providing a complete list of every single verse that could have been cited. Verses are listed under the following headings, interspersed with our comments:

- Titles of Jesus
- Old Testament References
- New Testament References

TITLES OF JESUS

The titles (or names) of Jesus are too numerous to list here. For the purpose of this book, we have restricted our choice to the titles referring to his deity and have ordered them according to their relationship to one another rather than their alphabetical order. This enables you to better appreciate the impact of who Jesus really is. Furthermore, we have included verses from both Old and New Testaments when both refer to the same title.

ROCK

In the Old Testament, YHWH is spoken of as the Rock

"For I [Moses] proclaim the name of the LORD: Ascribe greatness to our <u>God</u>. He <u>is the Rock</u>, His work is perfect; for all His ways are justice, a God of truth and without injustice; righteous and upright is He." (Deuteronomy 32:3-4; see also Deuteronomy 32:15, 18)

King David said: *"As for God, His way is perfect; the word of the LORD is proven; He is a shield to all who trust in Him. For who is God, except the LORD? And <u>who is a rock, except our God?</u>"* (2 Samuel 32:31-32)

In the New Testament, JESUS is revealed to be that same Rock

Prior to his life on earth, Jesus was the spiritual Rock:
"And all drank the same spiritual drink. For they drank of that <u>spiritual Rock</u> that followed them, and that <u>Rock was Christ</u>." (1 Corinthians 10:4)

During his life on earth, Jesus became the rock on which HE built his church:
"Simon Peter answered and said, "<u>You are the Christ, the Son of the living God</u>." Jesus answered and said to him, "Blessed are you, Simon Bar-Jonah, for flesh and blood has not revealed this to you, but My Father who is in heaven. And I also say to you that you are Peter, and <u>on this rock</u> [i.e. that Jesus is the Christ, the Son of the Living God] I will build My church, and the gates of Hades shall not prevail against it." (Matthew 16:16-18)

But to unbelieving Israel, Jesus became a 'Rock of Offence.' The Bible puts it this way:

> *"As it is written: "BEHOLD, I LAY IN ZION A STUMBLING STONE AND <u>ROCK OF OFFENSE</u>, AND WHOEVER BELIEVES ON HIM WILL NOT BE PUT TO SHAME."* (Romans 9:3)

MIGHTY GOD – EVERLASTING FATHER – PRINCE OF PEACE

(Another valid translation of 'Everlasting Father' is 'Father of Eternity')

> *"For unto us a Child is born, unto us a Son is given; and the government will be upon His shoulder. And His name will be called Wonderful, Counselor, <u>Mighty God</u>, <u>Everlasting Father</u> [or Father of Eternity], <u>Prince of Peace</u>."*
> (Isaiah 9:6)

Note: the name *Jehovah Shalom* (translated 'the LORD is Peace') appears in Judges 6:24 where it is attributed to Yahweh (Jehovah).

ALPHA AND OMEGA – THE ALMIGHTY

Four times Jesus is clearly identified by this title in the last book of the Bible, the book of Revelation:

> *"I am the <u>Alpha and the Omega</u>, the Beginning and the End," says the Lord, "who is and who was and who is to come, the <u>Almighty</u>."* (Revelation 1:8)

> *"I am the <u>Alpha and the Omega</u>, the First and the Last," and, "What you see, write in a book and send it to the seven churches which are in Asia…"* (Revelation 1:11)

> *"And He said to me, "It is done! I am the <u>Alpha and the Omega</u>, the Beginning and the End. I will give of the fountain of the water of life freely to him who thirsts."* (Revelation 21:6)

> *"I am the <u>Alpha and the Omega</u>, the Beginning and the End, the First and the Last."* (Revelation 22:13)

IMAGE OF GOD

> "...whose minds the god of this age has blinded, who do not believe, lest the light of the gospel of the glory of <u>Christ</u>, who is the <u>image of God</u>, should shine on them." (2 Corinthians 4:4)

Jesus – The Image of God

IMMANUEL (GOD IS WITH US)

> "Therefore the Lord Himself will give you a sign: Behold, the virgin shall conceive and bear a Son, and shall call His name <u>Immanuel</u>." (Isaiah 7:14)

"I AM"

> "Jesus said to them, "Most assuredly, I say to you, before Abraham was, <u>I AM</u>." (John 8:58)

Jesus is referring here to the great 'I Am,' the Yahweh/ Jehovah of the Old Testament. We will say more about this under New Testament References/ The Gospel of John.

Jesus – The Great "I AM"

GOD

In the following six passages Jesus is acknowledged as God:

> "In the beginning was the Word, and the Word was with God, and <u>the Word was God</u>." (John 1:1)

> "And Thomas answered and said to Him, "My Lord and <u>my God</u>!" (John 20:28)

> "...of whom [speaking of the Israelites] are the fathers and from whom, according to the flesh, Christ came, who is over all, the <u>eternally blessed God</u>. Amen." (Romans 9:5)

"…looking for the blessed hope and glorious appearing of our <u>great God and Savior</u> Jesus Christ." (Titus 2:13)

"But to the Son He [the Father] says: "YOUR THRONE, O <u>GOD</u>, IS FOREVER AND EVER; A SCEPTER OF RIGHTEOUSNESS IS THE SCEPTER OF YOUR KINGDOM." (Hebrews 1:8)

"And we know that the Son of God has come and has given us an understanding, that we may know Him who is true; and we are in Him who is true, in His Son <u>Jesus Christ</u>. This is the <u>true God and eternal life</u>." (1 John 5:20)

LORD OF ALL

"The word which God sent to the children of Israel, preaching peace through Jesus Christ—He is <u>Lord of all</u>." (Acts 10:36)

LORD OF GLORY

"…which none of the rulers of this age knew; for had they known, they would not have crucified the <u>Lord of glory</u>." (1 Corinthians 2:8)

LORD OF LORDS

Referring to Jesus:

"Now out of His mouth goes a sharp sword, that with it He should strike the nations. And He Himself will rule them with a rod of iron. He Himself treads the winepress of the fierceness and wrath of Almighty God. And He has on His robe and on His thigh a name written: KING OF KINGS AND <u>LORD OF LORDS</u>." (Revelation 19:15-16)

Referring to Yahweh/Jehovah:

"For the LORD your God is God of gods and <u>Lord of lords</u>, the great God, mighty and awesome, who shows no partiality nor takes a bribe." (Deuteronomy 10:17) Compare the following New Testament verse:

"I urge you in the sight of God…that you keep this commandment without spot, blameless until our Lord Jesus Christ's appearing,

> which He will manifest in His own time, He who is the blessed and only Potentate, the King of kings and <u>Lord of lords</u>, who alone has immortality, dwelling in unapproachable light, whom no man has seen or can see, to whom be honor and everlasting power. Amen." (1 Timothy 6:13-14)

LORD OUR RIGHTEOUSNESS

The following prophecy refers to Jesus reigning over his kingdom. He will do so when he returns to earth and will then be called Jehovah-tsidkenu. This is one of the titles given to him as the promised Messiah and is translated 'The Lord, our Righteousness':

> "In His days Judah will be saved, And Israel will dwell safely; now this is His name by which He will be called: <u>THE LORD OUR RIGHTEOUSNESS</u>. (Jeremiah 23:6)

REDEEMER

The Old Testament frequently speaks of the LORD God (Yahweh/Jehovah) as the Redeemer of his people. Here is one example:

> "All flesh shall know that I, the LORD, am your Savior, and your <u>Redeemer</u>, the Mighty One of Jacob." (Isaiah 49:26)

The New Testament is more specific in that it clearly shows Jesus Christ to be this redeemer:

> "<u>Christ has redeemed</u> us from the curse of the law, having become a curse for us for it is written, "CURSED IS EVERYONE WHO HANGS ON A TREE." (Galatians 3:13)

> "...knowing that you were not <u>redeemed</u> with corruptible things, like silver or gold, from your aimless conduct received by tradition from your fathers, but <u>with the precious blood of Christ</u>, as of a lamb without blemish and without spot. He indeed was fore-ordained before the foundation of the world, but was manifest in these last times for you." (1 Peter 1:18-20)

> "And they sang a new song [to the lamb/Jesus in the midst of the throne], saying: "You are worthy to take the scroll, and to open its

seals; for You were slain, and have <u>redeemed</u> us to God <u>by Your blood</u> out of every tribe and tongue and people and nation." (Revelation 5:9)

Jesus – The Redeemer

GOD THE SAVIOR

Referring to Jesus:

"For unto you is born this day in the city of David a <u>Savior, which is Christ the Lord</u>." (Luke 2:11)

To <u>God our Savior</u>, who alone is wise, be glory and majesty, dominion and power, both now and forever. Amen. (Jude 1:25)

The context here shows that Jude is speaking of Jesus, who is being addressed as 'God and Savior.'

Referring to what Yahweh/Jehovah says about himself:

"I, even I, am the LORD, and besides Me there is no <u>Savior</u>." (Isaiah 43:11)

"And there is no other God besides Me, a just God and a <u>Savior</u>; there is none besides Me." (Isaiah 45:21)

"All flesh shall know that I, the LORD, am your <u>Savior</u>, and your Redeemer, the Mighty One of Jacob." (Isaiah 49:26)

"Yet I am the LORD your God ever since the land of Egypt, and you shall know no God but Me; for there is <u>no Savior besides Me</u>." (Hosea 13:4)

Note: In the Old Testament, Jehovah makes it clear that he is the only savior, and yet the New Testament declares Jesus to be the only savior.

Jesus – God the Savior

WORD

"In the beginning was the Word, and the Word was with God, and the Word was God ... And the Word became flesh and dwelt among us, and we beheld His glory, the glory as of the only begotten of the Father, full of grace and truth." (John 1:1,14)

WORD OF LIFE

"That which was from the beginning, which we have heard, which we have seen with our eyes, which we have looked upon, and our hands have handled, concerning the Word of life." (1 John 1:1)

Jesus – The Word of Life

WORD OF GOD

"He was clothed with a robe dipped in blood, and His name is called The Word of God." (Revelation 19:13)

AMEN

"And to the angel of the church of the Laodiceans write, 'These things says the Amen, the Faithful and True Witness, the Beginning of the creation of God." (Revelation 3:14)

Note: the word 'Beginning' in this passage would be better translated in the sense of 'the first place of rank,' i.e. *chief, magistrate, principality, power or rule.* Jesus was never created. He was (and still is) the creator. He is *the Beginning of the creation of God* in the sense of bringing creation into being.

Jesus – The Amen

▪ OLD TESTAMENT REFERENCES

The Bible has a 'red thread' running right through it: the Lord Jesus Christ. The Old Testament points forward to him in shadowy types whereas the New Testament fully declares him in all of his glory. Creation and redemption are the two main themes of Scripture, and the Lord Jesus Christ is involved in both. Let us first read a few of many Old Testament passages that equate Jesus with God.

A messenger prepares the path for God/Jesus

In the Old Testament, God said he would send a messenger to prepare the way for himself:

> *"Behold, I send My messenger, and he will prepare the way <u>before Me</u>. And the Lord, whom you seek, will suddenly come to His temple, even the Messenger of the covenant, in whom you delight. Behold, He is coming," says the LORD of hosts."* (Malachi 3:1)

> *"The voice of one crying in the wilderness: "Prepare <u>the way of the LORD</u>; Make straight in the desert a highway <u>for our God</u>."*(Isaiah 40:3)

In the New Testament, this messenger is revealed to be John the Baptist, who points to Jesus as that LORD, saying,

> *"I am THE VOICE OF ONE CRYING IN THE WILDERNESS: MAKE STRAIGHT THE WAY OF THE <u>LORD</u>, as the prophet Isaiah said."* (John 1:23)

Note: John used the Greek word 'kurios' for 'LORD,' which refers to someone who has supreme authority.

God/Jesus was pierced

> *"And I [the LORD God] will pour on the house of David and on the inhabitants of Jerusalem the Spirit of grace and supplication; then <u>they will look on Me whom they pierced</u>. Yes, they will mourn for*

Him as one mourns for his only son, and grieve for Him as one grieves for a firstborn." (Zechariah 12:10)

Note: this is God speaking about himself in a prophecy concerning Jesus.
The prophecy points to the second coming of Christ. Did you notice that God refers to himself as having been pierced, whereas the New Testament reveals the pierced one to be Jesus?

Jesus is foretold to be THE LORD OUR RIGHTEOUSNESS

"Behold, the days are coming," says the LORD, "That I will raise to David a Branch of righteousness. A King shall reign and prosper, and execute judgment and righteousness in the earth. In His days Judah will be saved, And Israel will dwell safely. Now this is His name by which He will be called: <u>THE LORD [Yahweh] OUR RIGHTEOUSNESS</u>." (Jeremiah 23:5-6)

This passage refers to Jesus who will reign as king over Israel at his second coming. In his humanity he is referred to as a descendant of David, yet in his deity he receives a name which applies to God alone: 'Yahweh/Jehovah Our Righteousness.' In this passage, one LORD (Yahweh/Jehovah) says that he will raise up a king who will also be called LORD (Yahweh/ Jehovah). This can only be true if God the Father is talking about God the Son, Jesus Christ.

God's glory is bestowed on Jesus

"I am the LORD [Yahweh], that is My name; And <u>My glory I will not give to another</u>, nor My praise to carved images." (Isaiah 42:8)

Yahweh declared that he would not give his glory to anyone else, and yet Jesus shared that glory before the world existed, and he will share it again:

"And now, O Father, glorify Me together with Yourself, with the <u>glory which I had with You before the world was</u>." (John 17:5)

Jesus also predicted that he would come again in that glory:

> *"For whoever is ashamed of Me and My words in this adulterous and sinful generation, of him the Son of Man also will be ashamed <u>when He comes in the glory of His Father</u> with the holy angels."* (Mark 8:38)

God anoints God (Jesus)

> In the Psalms we read: *"Your throne, O God, is forever and ever; a scepter of righteousness is the scepter of Your kingdom. You love righteousness and hate wickedness. Therefore <u>God, Your God, has anointed You</u> with the oil of gladness more than Your companions."* (Psalm 45:6-7)

Adding the Hebrew 'Elohim' (plural noun for God) to this verse wherever it occurs, helps to clarify its grammatical structure and meaning:

> *"Your throne, O God* [Elohim], *is forever and ever; a scepter of righteousness is the scepter of Your kingdom. You love righteousness and hate wickedness; Therefore God* [another Elohim], *Your God* [the Elohim of the first-mentioned Elohim], *has anointed You* [the first-mentioned Elohim] *with the oil of gladness more than Your companions."* (Psalm 45:6-7)

It now becomes clearer that the Psalmist by way of prophecy addresses the first Elohim (who is Jesus) and says, *"Your throne is forever, and righteousness is the sceptre of your kingdom."* Then he states that another Elohim (again the plural noun, but now referring to the Father) has anointed the first Elohim (Jesus). We know this to be true because the same passage is quoted by the writer of Hebrews, and here the Son is addressed as God by the Father:

> *"But <u>to the Son</u> He* [the Father] *says: "YOUR THRONE, O GOD, IS FOREVER AND EVER; A SCEPTER OF RIGHTEOUSNESS IS THE SCEPTER OF YOUR KINGDOM."* (Hebrews 1:8)

The overall context of Hebrews 1:5-13 makes the meaning more obvious: deity is addressing deity, i.e. God the Father is speaking to God the Son. This verse will be discussed further in the next section (New Testament References/Letter to the Hebrews)

Divinity and humanity are combined in Jesus

> *"But you, <u>Bethlehem</u> Ephrathah, though you are little among the thousands of Judah, yet out of you shall come forth to Me the One to be Ruler in Israel, whose goings forth are from of old, <u>from everlasting</u>."* (Micah 5:2)

This passage is also quoted in Matthew 2:6. It names the birth place of Jesus as Bethlehem and at the same time confirms that he existed prior to his birth, from everlasting, eternal, without beginning. Only God has no beginning! And so, at the incarnation of Jesus, a human nature was added to his eternally divine nature. This is how God became flesh and dwelt with mankind for about 33 years.

▪ NEW TESTAMENT REFERENCES

We have finally arrived at the New Testament where we find many more passages referring to the deity of our Lord Jesus Christ. Most of them are listed without further explanation because they speak for themselves. For the purpose of oversight, we have grouped them in order of their occurrence, not in order of their theological importance, and the Gospel of John has received its own heading because of the large number of relevant verses it contains:

- *INTRODUCTION TO THE GOSPELS*
- *SYNOPTIC GOSPELS (Matthew, Mark, Luke)*
- *GOSPEL OF JOHN*
- *STATEMENTS BY PAUL*
- *STATEMENTS BY PETER*
- *HEBREWS*
- *REVELATION*

INTRODUCTION TO THE GOSPELS

Before we start, it is helpful to remember that the writers of the gospels were inspired by God to write what they did: "*All Scripture is given by inspiration of God, and is profitable for doctrine, for reproof, for correction, for instruction in righteousness,*" (2 Timothy 3:16). It is by God's guidance that they portrayed the Lord Jesus Christ from four different perspectives, each predicted in the Old Testament where Jesus is called 'the Branch.' Have you ever wondered why? A branch cannot produce itself; it grows out of a rootstock; it has a source. It naturally grows from that source and retains its nature. Therefore the word 'branch' in the Old Testament is often used in reference to 'parentage' or genealogy, and also as a title for Jesus.

MATTHEW introduces Jesus as 'The Branch of David' (Jeremiah 23:5), the lion-like **King of Israel** who, according to the flesh, is a true descendent of the royal line of King David.

MARK shows Jesus as 'Jehovah's Servant, the Branch' (Zechariah 3:8), who does the will of his Father. Brought forth by Yahweh, he is of the same rootstock but **takes on the role of a servant**: *"But made Himself of no reputation, taking the form of a bondservant, and coming in the likeness of men."* (Philippians 2:7)

LUKE portrays Jesus as 'The Man Whose Name Is the Branch' (Zechariah 6:12) and highlights him as the **Son of Man**.

JOHN finally reveals Jesus as 'The Branch of Jehovah' (Isaiah 4:2), i.e. the **Son of God** – deity from deity. Because this gospel focuses on Jesus as 'God in flesh,' it contains the most number of relevant passages and receives its own heading.

 SYNOPTIC GOSPELS

MATTHEW

"BEHOLD, THE VIRGIN SHALL BE WITH CHILD, AND BEAR A SON, AND THEY SHALL CALL HIS NAME IMMANUEL," which is translated, "God with us." (Matthew 1:23)

Note: this is a quote from Isaiah's prophecy, *"Therefore the Lord Himself will give you a sign: Behold, the virgin shall conceive and bear a Son, and shall call His name Immanuel."* (Isaiah 7:14)

And Jesus came and spoke to them, saying, "All authority has been given to Me in heaven and on earth. Go therefore and make disciples of all the nations, baptizing them in the name [singular] of the Father and of the Son and of the Holy Spirit, teaching them to observe all things that I have commanded you; and lo, I am with you always, even to the end of the age." Amen. (Matthew 28:18-20)

MARK

"Whoever receives one of these little children in My name receives Me; and whoever receives Me, receives not Me but Him who sent Me."(Mark 9:37)

LUKE

And the angel answered and said to her, "The Holy Spirit will come upon you, and the power of the Highest will overshadow you; therefore, also, that Holy One who is to be born will be called the Son of God. (Luke 1:35)

When Jesus was tried before the council of chief priests and scribes, they said: *"If You are the Christ, tell us."* But He said to them, *"If I tell you, you will by no means believe. And if I also ask you, you will by no means answer Me or let Me go. Hereafter the Son of Man will sit on the right hand of the power of God."* Then they all said, *"Are You then the Son of God?"* So He said to them, *"You rightly say that I am."* (Luke 22:67-70)

 GOSPEL OF JOHN

As previously mentioned, John primarily focuses on Jesus as the Son of God, the 'Branch of Jehovah' (Isaiah 4:2). The apostle highlights his deity, which makes this gospel a treasure trove for relevant Bible passages.

John fittingly begins with the history of Jesus as God. We have already discussed the first three verses in Part 2 of this book, but it won't hurt to read them again. In all, we will point out **nine major reasons** why Jesus is the Son of God and therefore truly God:

1. Jesus the 'Word' was God the creator who became flesh

"In the beginning was the Word, and the Word was with God, and the Word was God." (John 1:1)

"All things were made through Him [Jesus], and without Him nothing was made that was made." (John 1:3) Compare also Colossians 1:16.

"He was in the world, and the world was made through Him, and the world did not know Him. He came to His own, and His own did not receive Him. But as many as received Him, to them He gave the right to become children of God, to those who believe in His name: who were born, not of blood, nor of the will of the flesh, nor of the will of man, but of God. And <u>the Word became flesh</u> and dwelt among us, and we beheld His glory, the glory as of the only begotten of the Father, full of grace and truth." (John 1:10-14)

2. Jesus has declared God

"No one has seen God at any time. The only begotten Son, who is in the bosom of the Father, He has <u>declared</u> Him." (John 1:18)

3. Jesus has power to take away the sin of the world

"The next day John saw Jesus coming toward him, and said, "Behold! The <u>Lamb of God [Jesus] who takes away the sin of the world</u>!" (John 1:29)

Note: The Jews knew very well that only God can forgive sins, so when Jesus told the paralytic man in Mark 2:5 that his sins were forgiven, they responded

"Why does this Man speak blasphemies like this? <u>Who can forgive sins but God alone</u>?" (Mark 2:7)

4. Jesus is the giver of life, the judge, the one to be honoured equally with the Father

In his own words: *"For as the Father raises the dead and gives life to them, even so <u>the Son gives life to whom He will</u>. For the Father judges no one, but has committed <u>all judgment to the Son</u>, that <u>all should honor the Son just as they honor the Father</u>. He who does not honor the Son does not honor the Father who sent Him."* (John 5:21-23)

"For as the Father has life in Himself, so He has granted the Son to have life in Himself, and has given Him authority to execute judgment also, because He is the Son of Man." (John 5:26-27)

5. Jesus, Spirit and Father share the same resurrection power

Resurrection Power of the Son

Jesus had power to raise himself:

"*I am the resurrection and the life. He who believes in Me, though he may die, he shall live.*" (John 11:35)

"*Jesus answered and said to them, "Destroy this temple, and in three days I will raise it up.*" but "*He was speaking of the temple of His body.*" (John 2:19,21)

"*Therefore My Father loves Me, because I lay down My life that I may take it again. No one takes it from Me, but I lay it down of Myself. I have power to lay it down, and I have power to take it again. This command I have received from My Father.*" (John 10:17-18)

Resurrection Power of the Holy Spirit

The Holy Spirit took part in raising Jesus from the dead:

"[Jesus was] *declared to be the Son of God with power according to the Spirit of holiness, by the resurrection from the dead.*" (Romans 1:4)

"*Christ also suffered once for sins, the just for the unjust, that He might bring us to God, being put to death in the flesh but made alive by the Spirit,*" (1 Peter 3:18)

The Holy Spirit will also raise believers from the dead:

"*But if the Spirit of Him who raised Jesus from the dead dwells in you, He who raised Christ from the dead will also give life to your mortal bodies through His Spirit who dwells in you.*" (Romans 8:11)

Resurrection Power of God the Father

Peter and Paul both testified that God raised Jesus from the dead:

"*…whom God raised up, having loosed the pains of death, because it was not possible that He should be held by it.*" (Acts 2:24)

"*The God of our fathers raised up Jesus whom you murdered by hanging on a tree.*" (Acts 5:30)

"But if there is no resurrection of the dead, then Christ is not risen. And if Christ is not risen, then our preaching is empty and your faith is also empty. Yes, and we are found false witnesses of God, because we have testified of <u>God </u>that <u>He raised up Christ</u>, whom He did not raise up—if in fact the dead do not rise. Yes, and we are found false witnesses of God, because we have testified of God that He raised up Christ." (1 Corinthians 15:13-15)

We can therefore conclude that all three persons of the Godhead were involved in raising Jesus from the dead, making all three equal in power.

6. Jesus is one with the Father

"Philip said to Him, "Lord, show us the Father, and it is sufficient for us." Jesus said to him, "Have I been with you so long, and yet you have not known Me, Philip? <u>He who has seen Me has seen the Father</u>; so how can you say, 'Show us the Father'?" (John 14:8-9)

"I and My Father are one." (John 10:30)

Some falsely teach that Jesus and the Father are one merely in purpose, but the Jews understood very well what Jesus was saying, i.e. that he claimed to be God. They considered this to be blasphemy and took up stones to stone him (John 10:31-33). Leviticus 24:16 commanded death by stoning for those who blaspheme the Name of the Lord. Blasphemy is a serious matter.

7. Jesus accepts the title of God

"And Thomas answered and said to Him, "<u>My Lord and my God</u>!" (John 20:28) Notice that Jesus did not object!

John later confirmed this truth when he wrote in 1 John 5:20:

"And we know that the Son of God has come and has given us an understanding, that we may know Him who is true; and we are in Him who is true, in <u>His Son Jesus Christ. This is the true God and eternal life</u>."

8. Jesus shares the glory of the Father

"And now, O Father, glorify Me together with Yourself, with the glory which I had with You before the world was." (John 17:5)

"Father, I desire that they also whom You gave Me may be with Me where I am, that they may behold My glory which You have given Me; for You loved Me before the foundation of the world." (John 17:24)

Considering the fact that Jesus shared God's glory before the world was, it is no surprise that he declared himself to be the great 'I AM,' the LORD who in the Old Testament appeared to Moses.

9. Jesus claims equality with God as the "I AM"

In the Old Testament, YHWH God called himself "I AM":

"And God said to Moses, "I AM WHO I AM." And He said, "Thus you shall say to the children of Israel, 'I AM has sent me to you.'" (Exodus 3:14)

In the New Testament, Jesus claimed that name for himself:

"Jesus said to them, "Most assuredly, I say to you, before Abraham was, I AM." Then they took up stones to throw at Him; but Jesus hid Himself and went out of the temple, going through the midst of them, and so passed by." (John 8:58-59)

The Jews correctly understood that Jesus claimed to be the LORD of the Old Testament and once again took up stones to stone him. But because he actually was who he claimed to be, Jesus had the power to become invisible and walk right through the crowds.

Seven times, Jesus referred to his identity as the great 'I AM' in fulfilment of Old Testament typology. The following passages begin with the statements of Jesus in the Gospel of John and are followed by passages from the Old Testament (OT) where God, the LORD, is spoken of as fulfilling the same role.

THE SEVEN "I AM's" IN THE GOSPEL OF JOHN

- *"I am the bread of life"*

    NT: *"Most assuredly, I [Jesus] say to you, Moses did not give you the bread from heaven, but My Father gives you the true bread from heaven. For the bread of God is He who comes down from heaven and gives life to the world." Then they said to Him, "Lord, give us this bread always." And Jesus said to them, "<u>I am the bread of life</u>. He who comes to Me shall never hunger, and he who believes in Me shall never thirst."* (John 6:32-35)

    OT: *"So when the children of Israel saw [the manna], they said to one another, "What is it?" ... And Moses said to them, "This is the bread which the LORD has given you to eat."* (Exodus 16:15)

- *"I am the light of the world"*

    NT: *"Then Jesus spoke to them again, saying, "<u>I am the light of the world</u>. He who follows Me shall not walk in darkness, but have the light of life." The Pharisees therefore said to Him, "You bear witness of Yourself; Your witness is not true." Jesus answered and said to them, "Even if I bear witness of Myself, My witness is true, for I know where I came from and where I am going; but you do not know where I come from and where I am going."* (John 8:12-14)

    OT: *"The sun shall no longer be your light by day, nor for brightness shall the moon give light to you; but the LORD [Jehovah] will be to you an everlasting light, and your God your glory."* (Isaiah 60:19)

- *"I am the door"*

    NT: *"Then Jesus said to them again, "Most assuredly, I say to you, <u>I am the door</u> of the sheep."* (John 10:7)

    Jesus is the door through which his sheep (people) can enter into communion with God. In the Old Testament, it was the door of the tabernacle where God met with man:

OT: *"So Moses and Aaron went … to the door of the tabernacle of meeting, and they fell on their faces. And the glory of the LORD appeared to them.* (Num. 20:6)

And it came to pass, when Moses entered the tabernacle, that the pillar of cloud descended and stood at the door of the tabernacle, and the LORD talked with Moses." (Exodus 33:9)

➢ *"I am the good shepherd"*

NT: *"I am the good shepherd. The good shepherd gives His life for the sheep.* (John 10:11)

OT: *"Hear the word of the LORD, O nations, and declare it in the isles afar off, and say, 'He who scattered Israel will gather him, and keep him as a shepherd does his flock.' (Jeremiah 31:10)*

The LORD is my shepherd; I shall not want. (Psalm 23:1)

➢ *"I am the resurrection and the life"*

NT: *"Jesus said to her, "I am the resurrection and the life. He who believes in Me, though he may die, he shall live. "* (John 1:25)

NT: *"All things were made through Him* [Jesus], *and without Him nothing was made that was made. "* (John 1:3) / Compare also Colossians 1:16.

OT: *"And the LORD God* [Jehovah, the self-existent or eternal] *formed man of the dust of the ground, and breathed into his nostrils the breath of life; and man became a living being."* (Genesis 2:7)

➢ *"I am the way, the truth, and the life"*

NT: *"Jesus said to him, "I am the way, the truth, and the life. No one comes to the Father except through Me."* (John 14:6)

OT: *"The voice of one crying in the wilderness: "Prepare the way of the LORD; Make straight in the desert a highway for our God."* (Isaiah 40:3) This prophecy is quoted in all four gospels and each time refers to Jesus as being that way. (Matthew 3:3; Mark 1:3; Luke 3:4; John 1:23)

"For the LORD is good; His mercy is everlasting, and His <u>truth</u> endures to all generations." (Psalm 100:5)

> *"I am the true vine"*

NT: *"<u>I am the true vine</u>, and My Father is the vinedresser. Every branch in Me that does not bear fruit He takes away; and every branch that bears fruit He prunes, that it may bear more fruit."* (John 15:1-2)

Explanation of Old Testament Typology:
The nation of Israel was a vine planted by Yahweh, but it turned out to be unfaithful and unfruitful. Now Jesus speaks of himself as the true vine, the faithful and fruitful one. He is the one who provides life-giving sap to his 'branches' (all believers abiding in him), whose purpose it is to bear fruit. Jesus is the giver of life and fruit (which is God's power alone) while the Father is the gardener, tending the branches who receive their life from the vine.

 STATEMENTS BY PAUL

Paul believed that Jesus was God. His letters to the early churches and his statements in the book of Acts provide many references to Jesus as God. We will group this evidence under **six headings**:

1. Salvation is of God and salvation is of Jesus

The apostle Paul certainly believed that Jesus was God. He often cited Old Testament passages about Jehovah/God and applied them to the Lord Jesus Christ. One such example is a quote from the prophet Joel referring to the LORD [Jehovah], which Paul quoted in Romans 10:13, applying it to Jesus:

"And it shall come to pass that whoever calls on the name of the LORD [YHWH/Jehovah] shall be saved. For in Mount Zion and in Jerusalem there shall be deliverance, as the LORD [Jehovah] has said, among the remnant whom the LORD [YHWH/Jehovah] calls." (Joel 2:32) [Speaking of YHWH]

"For the Scripture says, "WHOEVER BELIEVES ON HIM WILL NOT BE PUT TO SHAME." and For "WHOEVER CALLS ON THE NAME OF THE LORD SHALL BE SAVED." (Romans 10:11,13) [Speaking of Jesus]

Peter goes a step further by emphasising that Jesus is the only savior:

"Nor is there salvation in any other, for there is no other name under heaven given among men by which we must be saved." (Acts 4:12)

This statement would certainly contradict many Old Testament passages unless it was true that Jesus is God or, as Paul expresses it, that he is part of the Godhead (Divinity):

"For since the creation of the world His invisible attributes are clearly seen, being understood by the things that are made, even His eternal power and Godhead [Divinity], so that they are without excuse," (Romans 1:20)

"For in Him dwells all the fullness of the Godhead [Divinity] bodily;" (Colossians 2:9)

2. Jesus is the image of the invisible God and also firstborn over all creation

"He is the image of the invisible God, the firstborn over all creation. For by Him all things were created that are in heaven and that are on earth, visible and invisible, whether thrones or dominions or principalities or powers. All things were created through Him and for Him. And He is before all things, and in Him all things consist. And He is the head of the body, the church, who is the beginning, the firstborn from the dead, that in all things He may have the pre-eminence. For it pleased the Father that in Him all the fullness should dwell, and by Him to reconcile all things to Himself, by Him, whether things on earth or things in heaven, having made peace through the blood of His cross." (Colossians 1:15-20)

Because this verse has been misinterpreted by some teachers, we have included the following excerpt from William MacDonald's Believer's Bible Commentary (ed. Art Farstad.

Thomas Nelson Publishers, Inc., Nashville, Tennessee, pp. 1993-1994) to help you stand firm against false teachers who claim that Jesus is a created being. MacDonald explains the expression "firstborn over all creation" (Colossians 1:15) according to correct biblical exegesis:

Excerpt from William MacDonald's Believer's Bible Commentary explaining Colossians 1:15-16

1:15 Christ is also **the firstborn over all creation**, or "of every created being." What does this mean? Some false teachers suggest that the Lord Jesus is Himself a created being, that He was the first Person whom God ever made. Some of them are even willing to go so far as to admit that He is the greatest creature ever to come from the hand of God. But nothing could be more directly contrary to the teaching of the word of God.

The expression "firstborn" has at least three different meanings in Scripture. In Luk 2:7, it is used in *a literal sense*, where Mary brought forth her firstborn Son. There it means that the Lord Jesus was the first Child to whom she gave birth. In Exo 4:22, on the other hand, it is used in *a figurative sense*. "Israel is My son, even My firstborn." In that verse there is no thought of an actual birth having taken place, but the Lord is using this word to describe the distinctive place which the nation of Israel had in His plans and purposes. Finally, in Psa 89:27, the word "firstborn" is used to designate *a place of superiority*, of supremacy, of uniqueness. There God says that He will make David His firstborn, higher than the kings of the earth. David was actually the last-born son of Jesse according to the flesh. But God determined to give him a place of unique supremacy, primacy, and sovereignty.

Is not that exactly the thought of Col 1:15 —**the firstborn over all creation**? The Lord Jesus Christ is God's unique Son. In one sense all believers are sons of God, but the Lord Jesus is God's Son in a way that is not true of any other. He existed before all creation and occupies a position of supremacy over it. His is the rank of eminence and dominion. The expression **firstborn over all creation** has nothing to do with birth here. It simply means that He is God's Son by an eternal relationship. It is a title of priority of *position*, and not simply one of time.

1:16 False teachers use verse 15 (especially in the KJV) to teach that the Lord Jesus was a created being. Error can usually be refuted from the very passage of Scripture which the cultists use. That is the case here. Verse 16 states conclusively that the Lord Jesus is not a creature, but the very Creator…

Paul goes to great lengths to emphasize that **all things were created through** Christ, whether things **in heaven**, or things **on earth**. This leaves no loopholes for anyone to suggest that although He created some things, He Himself was created originally.

The apostle then goes on to state that the Lord's creation included things **visible and** things **invisible**. The word **visible** needs no explanation, but doubtless the Apostle Paul realized that when he said **invisible** he would arouse our curiosity. Therefore, he proceeds to give a break-down of what he means by things **invisible**. They include **thrones, dominions, principalities**, and **powers**. We believe that these terms refer to angelic beings, although we cannot distinguish between the different ranks of these intelligent beings (who were created by Jesus).~ End of Quote

3. Jesus holds the fullness of the Godhead and all power

"In Him [Jesus] *dwells all the fullness of the Godhead bodily."* (Colossians 2:9)

The Greek for Godhead is theotēs, meaning *divinity:* all of the *Godhead* in a man's body, or all of *divinity* in a man's body. Paul uses the same word when he speaks of God's eternal power in his letter to the Romans:

"…because what may be known of God is manifest in them, for God has shown it to them. For since the creation of the world His invisible attributes are clearly seen, being understood by the things that are made, even His eternal power and Godhead, so that they are without excuse." (Romans 1:19-20)

And because this Godhead, this full divinity, dwelt in Jesus, Paul could say,

"[Jesus] *will transform our lowly body that it may be conformed to His glorious body, according to the working by which He is able even to subdue all things to Himself."* (Philippians 3:21)

Just picture this: Jesus will transform us because he is able to SUBDUE ALL THINGS to himself. Only God has that power!

4. The church of God is the church of Jesus

Paul encouraged the Ephesian elders to take care of God's church, knowing he would not see them again after their last meeting:

"Therefore take heed to yourselves and to all the flock, among which the Holy Spirit has made you overseers, to shepherd <u>the church of God which He purchased with His own blood</u>." (Act 20:28)

Here God is identified as purchasing <u>his</u> church with <u>his own blood</u>, whilst we are clearly told in other passages that it was Jesus who built his church, and that he died to redeem it with his blood:

"And I [Jesus] also say to you that you are Peter, and on this rock [referring to verse 17, i.e. that Jesus is the Christ, the Son of the Living God] *I will build My church, and the gates of Hades shall not prevail against it."* (Matthew 16:18)

"In Him [Jesus] we have redemption through His blood, the forgiveness of sins, according to the riches of His grace." (Ephesians 1:7)

"But now in Christ Jesus you who once were far off have been brought near by the blood of Christ." (Ephesians 2:13)

In the following verses we see the same equation of God (speaking through Isaiah about himself) and Jesus (spoken about by Paul, who learned these truths directly from the Lord).

5. Every knee shall bow before YHWH and Jesus

Referring to YHWH/Yahweh/Jehovah:

"Look to Me, and be saved, all you ends of the earth! For <u>I am God, and there is no other</u>. I have sworn by Myself; the word has gone out of My mouth in righteousness, and shall not return, that <u>to Me every knee shall bow</u>, every tongue shall take an oath." (Isaiah 45:22-23)

Referring to Jesus:

> "Let this mind be in you which was also in Christ Jesus, who, being in the form of God, did not consider it robbery to be equal with God, but made Himself of no reputation, taking the form of a bondservant, and coming in the likeness of men. And being found in appearance as a man, He humbled Himself and became obedient to the point of death, even the death of the cross. Therefore God also has highly exalted Him and given Him the name which is above every name, that <u>at the name of Jesus every knee should bow</u>, of those in heaven, and of those on earth, and of those under the earth, and that every tongue should confess that Jesus Christ is Lord, to the glory of God the Father." (Philippians 2:5-11)

6. Paul believed that Jesus is God

Paul certainly believed that Jesus is God and summed up this mystery in his letters to Titus and Timothy:

> "...looking for the blessed hope and glorious appearing of our great <u>God and Savior Jesus Christ</u>, who gave Himself for us, that He might redeem us from every lawless deed and purify for Himself His own special people, zealous for good works." (Titus 2:13-14)

> "And without controversy great is the mystery of godliness: <u>God was</u> manifested in the flesh, justified in the Spirit, seen by angels, preached among the Gentiles, believed on in the world, received up in glory." (1Timothy 3:16)

STATEMENTS BY PETER

Peter also believed that Jesus is God

> "...[Jesus] *who has gone into heaven and is at the right hand of God, <u>angels and authorities and powers having been made subject to Him</u>."* (1 Peter 3:22)

> *"Simon Peter, a bondservant and apostle of Jesus Christ, to those who have obtained like precious faith with us by the righteousness of <u>our God and Savior Jesus Christ</u>: Grace and peace be multiplied to you in the knowledge of God and of Jesus our Lord, as <u>His divine power</u> has given to us all things that pertain to life and godliness."* (2 Peter 1:1-3)

In his sermon in Acts, chapter 2, Peter quoted from Psalm 110, which the Jews knew to be a messianic prediction:

> *"For David did not ascend into the heavens, but he says himself: 'THE LORD SAID TO MY LORD, "SIT AT MY RIGHT HAND, TILL I MAKE YOUR ENEMIES YOUR FOOTSTOOL."' "Therefore let all the house of Israel know assuredly that God has made this Jesus, whom you crucified, both Lord and Christ."* (Acts 2:34-36)

Jesus himself had questioned the Pharisees along the same lines, saying,

> *"What do you think about the Christ? Whose Son is He?" They said to Him, "The Son of David." He said to them, "How then does David in the Spirit call Him 'LORD,' saying: 'THE LORD SAID TO MY LORD, "SIT AT MY RIGHT HAND, TILL I MAKE YOUR ENEMIES YOUR FOOTSTOOL" '? If David then calls Him 'LORD,' how is He his Son?" And no one was able to answer Him a word, nor from that day on did anyone dare question Him anymore."* (Matthew 22:42-46)

How could the coming Messiah be both David's son and David's Lord? The answer: As God, Jesus existed before King David and was David's Lord. But when he came to earth as a man, he was born as a physical descendent of David and therefore became his son (Matthew 1 and Luke 3). The concept of one Lord speaking to another Lord appears again in the book of Hebrews.

 *HEBREWS*

God the Father addresses the Son as God

Throughout the Old Testament, God decreed that only He is to be worshipped. Yet in the following passage we read that He decreed that the angels should worship the risen Messiah, the Son of God, who is God!

> "*God, who at various times and in various ways spoke in time past to the fathers by the prophets, has in these last days spoken to us by His Son, whom He has appointed heir of all things, through whom also He made the worlds; who being the brightness of His glory and the express image of His person, and upholding all things by the word of His power, when He had by Himself purged our sins, sat down at the right hand of the Majesty on high, having become so much better than the angels, as He has by inheritance obtained a more excellent name than they. For to which of the angels did He ever say: "YOU ARE MY SON, TODAY I HAVE BEGOTTEN YOU"? And again: "I WILL BE TO HIM A FATHER, AND HE SHALL BE TO ME A SON"? But when He again brings the firstborn into the world, He says: "LET ALL THE ANGELS OF GOD WORSHIP HIM."* (Hebrews 1:1-6)

In the following verse, God [the Father] says of his Son [Jesus] that he is God, that he is the LORD who created earth and the heavens, and that he is the one who remains after his creation has perished:

> "*But to the Son He says: "YOUR THRONE, O GOD, IS FOREVER AND EVER; A SCEPTER OF RIGHTEOUSNESS IS THE SCEPTER OF YOUR KINGDOM. (Hebrews 1:8) And: "YOU, LORD, IN THE BEGINNING LAID THE FOUNDATION OF THE EARTH, AND THE HEAVENS ARE THE WORK OF YOUR HANDS. THEY WILL PERISH, BUT YOU REMAIN."* (Hebrews 1:10-11)

> "*But to which of the angels has He ever said: "SIT AT MY RIGHT HAND, TILL I MAKE YOUR ENEMIES YOUR FOOTSTOOL?"* (Hebrews 1:13)

Compare also another passage in Hebrews:

But this Man [Jesus Christ], after He had offered one sacrifice for sins forever, sat down at the right hand of God, from that time waiting till His enemies are made His footstool. (Hebrews 10:12-13)

 *REVELATION*

The risen Jesus identifies himself to his churches as God

"I am the <u>Alpha and the Omega</u>, the Beginning and the End," says the Lord, "who is and who was and who is to come, the Almighty." (Revelation 1:8) In context, this is Jesus Christ speaking.

"I am He who lives, and was dead, and behold, I am <u>alive forevermore</u>. Amen. And I have the <u>keys of Hades and of Death</u>." (Revelation 1:18)

"To the angel of the church of Ephesus write, 'These things says He who holds the seven stars in His right hand, who walks in the midst of the seven golden lampstands" (Revelation 2:1)

"He who has an ear, let him hear what <u>the Spirit</u> says to the churches. To him who overcomes <u>I will give to eat from the tree of life</u>, which is in the midst of the Paradise of God." (Revelation 2:7)

Note: in the preceding verse, we clearly see that Jesus and the Spirit are synonymous. Jesus is the one speaking, but he declares that it is the Spirit who is speaking to the churches.

"And to the angel of the church in Pergamos write, 'These things says He who has the <u>sharp two-edged sword</u>..." (Revelation 2:12)

You might like to compare this verse with Hebrews 4:12:

"For <u>the word of God is living and powerful, and sharper than any two-edged sword</u>, even to the division of soul and spirit, and of joints and marrow, and is a discerner of the thoughts and intents of the heart." (Hebrews 4:12)

> *"And to the angel of the church in Sardis write, 'These things says <u>He [Jesus] who has the seven Spirits of God</u> and the seven stars."* (Revelation 3:1)

Note: the 'seven Spirits of God' refer to the fullness of God's Holy Spirit, and this fullness of the Holy Spirit is said to belong to God and also to Jesus, proving once again that Jesus is God!

> *"And to the angel of the church in Philadelphia write, 'These things says He who is holy, He who is true, "HE WHO HAS THE KEY OF DAVID, HE WHO OPENS AND NO ONE SHUTS, AND SHUTS AND NO ONE OPENS"* (Revelation 3:7)

> *"And to the angel of the church of the Laodiceans write, 'These things says the Amen, the Faithful and True Witness, the Beginning of the creation of God."* (Revelation 3:14)

Note: the word '*Beginning*' here should be better translated as the first place of rank, i.e. *chief, magistrate, principality, power, rule.*

Jesus sits on the throne of God

In Revelation, chapter 4, we see seven Spirits of God, twenty-four elders and four living creatures around the throne of God.

> *The creatures are continually saying, "Holy, holy, holy, <u>Lord God Almighty</u>, who was and is and is to come!" Whenever the living creatures give glory and honor and thanks to Him who sits on the throne, who lives forever and ever, the twenty-four elders fall down before Him who sits on the throne and worship Him who lives forever and ever, and cast their crowns before the throne, "You are worthy, O Lord, To receive glory and honor and power; for <u>You created all things, and by Your will they exist and were created</u>."* (Revelation 4:8-11)

Could it be that the elders are addressing the Lord Jesus together with God the Father? We believe so. Compare the following verses:

> *"He [Jesus] is the image of the invisible God, the firstborn over all creation. For <u>by Him</u> [Jesus] <u>all things were created</u> that are in heaven and that are on earth, visible and invisible, whether thrones or*

dominions or principalities or powers. <u>All things were created through Him and for Him</u>." (Colossians 1:15-16)

"And I looked, and behold, in the midst of the throne and of the four living creatures, and in the midst of the elders, stood a <u>Lamb</u> [Jesus] as though it had been slain, <u>having</u> seven horns and seven eyes, which are <u>the seven Spirits of God sent out into all the earth</u>." (Revelation 5:6)

Note: the Lamb (Jesus) has the seven Spirits of God, i.e. the fullness of the Holy Spirit is His.

Jesus is Lord of Lords and King of Kings

Referring to Yahweh/Jehovah:

For the LORD your God is <u>God of gods and Lord of lords</u>, the great God, mighty and awesome, who shows no partiality nor takes a bribe. (Deuteronomy 10:17)

Referring to Jesus:

"Now out of His mouth goes a sharp sword, that with it He should strike the nations. And He Himself will rule them with a rod of iron. He Himself treads the winepress of the fierceness and wrath of Almighty God. And He has on His robe and on His thigh a name written: <u>KING OF KINGS AND LORD OF LORDS</u>. (Revelation 19:15-16)

This brings us to the end of our New Testament evidence proving Jesus to be fully God. What a fitting conclusion that he should be called King of Kings and Lords of Lords!

The Lord Jesus Christ: Fully God

Final Words from the Authors

Dear Reader,

We hope you have enjoyed your journey through the Bible and have come to know Jesus more intimately. May God bless you richly for seeking to know him better!

There is so much more we could have written about the Lord Jesus Christ. You may have expected us to point to his extraordinary miracles, for example, which undoubtedly displayed the power of God. We chose not to do so because miracles were God's specific sign to a nation that were looking for signs – Israel (see 1 Corinthians 1:22). Peter and John very aptly summed up their purpose in just two verses:

"Men of Israel, hear these words: Jesus of Nazareth, a Man attested by God to you by miracles, wonders, and signs which God did through Him in your midst, as you yourselves also know…" (Peter in Acts 2:22)

"And truly Jesus did many other signs in the presence of His disciples, which are not written in this book; but these are written that you may believe that Jesus is the Christ [Messiah], the Son of God, and that believing you may have life in His name." (Apostle John in John 20:30-31)

Life in his name – what a wonderful God we have! He loves human beings so much that he sent his Son to die for them and to pay the penalty for their sins with his own blood. If anyone believes in HIM – the biblical Lord Jesus Christ – their sins will be forgiven, and they will enter into a relationship with the all-powerful God who created the universe. How awesome is that! Isaac Watts once wrote, "Love so amazing, so divine, demands my soul, my life, my all." (Isaac Watts, *When I Survey the Wondrous Cross*)

We have shown you from the Bible that Jesus truly is Almighty God. He is God the Son, one of the three persons of the one and only God who is one in plurality. He took on flesh to become a man and received the name Jesus (meaning 'Yahweh is Salvation'). Yet even as a man, he had the fullness of God dwelling in him. That is why he was the only person on earth who was absolutely faultless and never sinned. And for this reason he alone was worthy to become the perfect sacrifice for the sins of the whole world. A mere man (or even an angel) would not have qualified.

You, too, can become a child of the Most High God if you believe that this biblical Jesus died for your sins, that he was buried, and that he rose again the third day (1 Corinthians 15:1-6).

We greet you with Christian love and hope to see you in eternity!

June and Margaret

RESOURCES

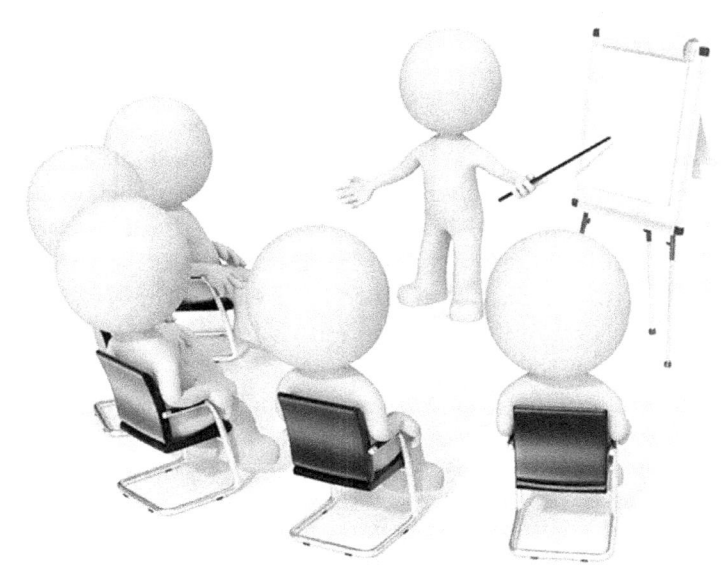

Answers to the John 1:1 Debate

By Margaret Lepke

Have you ever had Jehovah's Witnesses come to your door wanting to give you free Watchtower publications? We have, and they are usually very nice people. Well-meaning and sincere, they put in many hours to tell others about what they believe to be good news. Unfortunately, sincerity is not enough. It does not prove that their teachings are correct.

So what is the main controversy? It centres on the claim of **who Jesus is** and, by extension, on the correct translation of John 1:1. The New World Translation of the Holy Scriptures (which is their in-house translation and henceforth abbreviated as NWT), renders the first and most important verse of the Gospel of John as follows:

> "In [the] beginning the Word was, and the Word was with God, and the Word was ***a god***." NWT

Jehovah's Witnesses therefore claim that 'the Word' does not refer to the one and only God YHWH/Jehovah but to another, lesser god; a secondary god who was created by Jehovah and is one with him only in purpose. Thus they claim two deities of different rank. Christians cannot agree with this proposition because salvation hangs on the true identity of the Lord Jesus Christ. The New World Bible version is certainly not correct in its translation of John 1:1, and the following biblical and grammatical evidence will verify this. Unless otherwise noted, verses are from the NKJV.

~ Biblical Evidence

God does not lie, and he does not contradict himself. When he says, _"You shall have no other gods before me"_ in Exodus 20:3, he means it! God, being true to himself as the only potentate of the universe, is a jealous God and would never tolerate (and much less acknowledge) the existence of another, lesser god. This is what he says:

> "...you shall worship no other god, for the LORD, _whose name is Jealous_, is a jealous God." (Exodus 34:14)

The New World Translation omits his name and reads quite differently:

> *"You must not bow down to another god, for Jehovah is known for requiring exclusive devotion. Yes, he is a God who requires exclusive devotion."* NWT

God repeats this directive in Exodus and Deuteronomy:

> *"You shall not bow down to them* [other gods] *nor serve them, for <u>I, the LORD your God, am a jealous God</u>, visiting the iniquity of the fathers upon the children to the third and fourth generations of those who hate Me, but showing mercy to thousands, to those who love Me and keep My commandments."* (Exodus 20:5-6; the same is repeated in Deuteronomy 5:9-10)

This confirms that Jehovah God would certainly not acknowledge a lesser god as a legitimate god, and yet he calls his Son 'God':

> *"But <u>to the Son</u> He says: "<u>YOUR THRONE, O GOD</u>, IS FOREVER AND EVER; A SCEPTER OF RIGHTEOUSNESS IS THE SCEPTER OF YOUR KINGDOM."* (Hebrews 1:8)

Again, the NWT is quite contrary, producing a very different meaning:

> *"But <u>about the Son</u>, he says: "<u>God is your throne</u> forever and ever, and the scepter of your Kingdom is the scepter of uprightness."* NWT

For Jehovah God to call his Son 'God,' (which is the correct translation according to grammatical evidence presented under the next heading), the Son must be equally God and equal in power. This concept once again indicates God to be 'one in plurality,' something that is difficult for us to comprehend as it is a spiritual mystery. We simply believe it because God has revealed it to us through MANY scriptures in His Holy Word. Hebrews 1:8 is not the only verse that shows God to be one in plurality.

At the very beginning of the Bible, we find an interesting statement where God refers to himself as 'us,' (a plural identity) who created (in singular verb form) the universe:

> *"In the beginning God* [plural noun Elohim] *created the heavens and the earth."* (Genesis 1:1)
>
> *"Then God said, "Let Us make man in Our image, according to Our likeness; let them have dominion over the fish of the sea, over the birds of the air, and over the cattle, over all the earth and over every creeping thing that creeps on the earth."* (Genesis 1:26)

The same concept appears again in Isaiah where God says,

> *"Whom shall I send, and who will go for Us?"* (Isaiah 6:8)

Here Jehovah God actually uses the 'I' and 'Us' synonymously in the same sentence, presenting the concept of 'one God in plurality,' i.e. a God who exists in relationship with himself. This is supported by the fact that the Bible ascribes creation to both YHWH (Yahweh/ Jehovah) and Jesus; YHWH in the Old Testament, and Jesus in the New:

CREATOR – YHWH (Yahweh/Jehovah)

> *"I am the LORD, your Holy One, The Creator of Israel, your King."* (Isaiah 43:15)
>
> *"Have you not known? Have you not heard? The everlasting God, the LORD, The Creator of the ends of the earth, neither faints nor is weary. His understanding is unsearchable."* (Isaiah 40:28)

CREATOR – JESUS

> *"For by him [Jesus] all things were created, in the heavens and on the earth, things visible and things invisible, whether thrones or dominions or principalities or powers; all things have been created through him, and for him. He is before all things, and in him all things are held together. He is the head of the body, the assembly, who is the beginning, the firstborn from the dead; that in all things he might have the pre-eminence."* (Colossians 1:15-18)

We are told more than once that Jesus created the universe. In John's Gospel, for example, the apostle introduces his good news by stating that *'the Word was God.'* Then John continues to identify this *'Word'* with a male person (in John 1:3) through whom all things were created. This statement is repeated a little later in John 1:10-14 in a context that clearly points to Jesus as being not only this male *'Word'* but also the great creator of the universe who came to live among men who were able to witness his glory:

> *"All things were made through Him, and without Him nothing was made that was made."* (John 1:3)
>
> *"He was in the world, and the world was made through Him, and the world did not know Him. He came to His own, and His own did not receive Him. But as many as received Him, to them He gave the right to become children of God, to those who believe in His name: who were born, not of blood, nor of the will of the flesh, nor of the will of man, but of God. And the Word became flesh and dwelt among us, and we beheld His glory, the glory as of the only begotten of the Father, full of grace* ['divine favour' NWT] *and truth."* (John 1:10-14)

Not only does the Bible ascribe creation to Jesus, it also ascribes to him the power to sustain his creation:

> *"...who, being the brightness* [NWT: 'reflection'] *of His glory and the express image of His person, and <u>upholding all things by the word of His power</u>, when He had by Himself purged our sins* [NWT: 'had made a purification for our sins']*, sat down at the right hand of the Majesty on high, having become so much better than the angels, as He has by inheritance obtained a more excellent name than they."* (Hebrews 1:3-4)

Who else but God could sit at the right hand of the Majesty on high? Note that Jesus INHERITED a higher position than the angels. Angels are created beings, but the pre-existent Jesus was never an angel (as the Jehovah's Witnesses claim).

But how can God sit next to God if there is only one God? This is possible only if God is indeed one God existing in plurality, a concept described by many scholars as 'one Godhead including three persons: Father, Son and Holy Spirit.' If you would like to read more on this and see proof from the Bible, you can download a free, short eBook titled *Answers to the Trinity Debate*. Here is the link: www.biblicalpublications.org/ebooks.html (more information in our resource section on page 73).

~ *Grammatical Evidence*

Not only do we have biblical evidence, we also have grammatical evidence to refute the Watchtower translation of John 1:1. In everyday life, you may not think much about grammar, but when you want to translate something from one language to another without changing its meaning, grammar becomes very important.

It is the last part of John 1:1, namely *theos en ho logos,* that is disputed by Jehovah's Witnesses who claim that a lack of the article *ho* in front of *theos* should render this part of the sentence as *the Word was a god (with a small g).* In order to find out whether this is correct, we need to consider grammar.

It is true that the Greek word *theos (god)* appears in different contexts and is translated accordingly. It can (and usually does) refer to the Supreme Being God as revealed in Scripture, but it can also refer to false 'gods' (e.g. 1 Corinthians 8:5) and even to the devil as the 'god of this age' (see 2 Cor. 4:4). It is also true that the Greek definite article *ho (the)* often precedes *theos,* but it is likewise true that it does not always do so, depending on its grammatical position. In fact, in John 1:1 it should NOT precede *theos* as shown a little later.

First, let us look at a word-for-word translation from the Greek text:

En	archē	ēn	ho	Logos		
Ἐν	ἀρχῇ	ἦν	ὁ	Λόγος ,		
In [the]	beginning	was	the	Word		

kai	ho	Logos	ēn	pros	ton	Theon
καὶ	ὁ	Λόγος	ἦν	πρὸς	τὸν	Θεόν ,
and	the	Word	was	with	-	God

kai	Theos	ēn	ho	Logos		
καὶ	Θεὸς	ἦν	ὁ	Λόγος .		
and	God	was	the	Word		

Most English Bible translations read like this:

> *"In the beginning was the Word* [or, *the word already existed/was already there*] *and the Word was with God, and <u>the Word was God</u>."* (KJV, NKJV, NIRV, NIV, NLT, RV, WEB, Webster and others).

The last part of the sentence is turned around in English due to grammatical indications as explained on the following page.

Looking at the above Greek/English translation, we can see at a glance that the Greek *theos* occurs twice in this verse, and that the different endings of *theos* and *theon* are simply inflections to indicate sentence structure. Both times, the word occurs without the definite article, and grammatical rules require that both *theon* and *theos* should be translated identically, i.e. *'god'* or *'God.'*

The first occurrence (*'the Word was with God'*) undoubtedly refers to the one and only Almighty God. We find this rendering throughout the New Testament to refer to the God of the universe, the YHWH (Jehovah) of the Old Testament. There is therefore no plausible reason why the second occurrence should be translated in a different manner such as *'the Word was god' (with a small g)* to indicate a lesser god as Jehovah's Witnesses have done, or even as *'the Word was divine'*. Both times *theos* clearly refers to the same Jehovah God, even without a preceding definite article.

Since it is true that the definite article does in many cases precede *theos* elsewhere in the Bible when referring to Jehovah God, we need to ask why John choose NOT to include it here. The answer is surprisingly simple: for the sake of good grammar!

The Greek language uses inflections, which are (typically) word endings that change the form of a word to express a grammatical function or attribute such as tense, mood, person, number, case and gender. One must therefore look at noun endings to determine a subject.

In the latter part of John 1:1, however, we encounter two nouns with the same endings (*logos and theos*). This could be confusing if not resolved by placing a definite article only in front of the subject (*'Word'*), which is exactly what the apostle did to avoid misunderstanding. John made certain his readers understood that he meant to say, *'The Word was God'* (as it appears in our English translations) rather than *'God was the Word'* (as you see it on page 70 in the Greek/English word for word translation which does not consider grammatical structure).

Independent Greek scholars also agree that it is grammatically correct in this particular sentence for *theos* to lack the article *ho* because *theos* here is the predicate that precedes both the noun *logos* and the verb *en*. Hence they are agreed that this verse should be translated *"the Word was God,"* and the Greek word order is changed accordingly in the English language.

In summary, we can say with certainty that the Bible identifies Jesus to be the logos, the Word, the expression of God. We can also say that Jesus existed in the beginning with God and that he was God. He spoke all things into existence and even now holds all things together in himself. This clearly shows that he has always held all the power of God and that his statement in John 10:30 is perfectly true. Jesus and his Father are ONE in Godhead, not just one in purpose.

> *"I and (my/the) Father are one."*
>
> (John 10:30)

Note: the word 'my' (and in other translations 'the') does not exist in the original manuscripts and was added by the translators in order to complete the sentence.

1 John 1:1

Answers to the Trinity Debate

Was the Trinity invented by the early church?

Trying to understand a God who is beyond our comprehension is a difficult task. He has revealed himself to us in many ways, and yet we cannot fully comprehend everything about him. The concept of Trinity seeks to explain what can be known about God.

Many contend that this doctrine was invented by the early church, but that is not the case. It is true that early Christians did not have a Trinitarian doctrine set in stone, but from the very beginning they held to the deity of their Lord Jesus Christ. The influence of heresy finally forced their leaders to state more precisely what they believed and to defend their faith by way of argument.

We offer a short, free eBook that examines this debate in a nutshell. It sheds light on historical happenings before presenting evidence from Scripture to show that God truly exists as three in one.

FREE DOWNLOAD FROM
www.biblicalpublications.org/ebooks.html

Jesus Is Alive – And He Is Coming Back!

Have you studied the Bible concerning future events?
Have you heard about the fact that Jesus is coming back?
Are you excited at this prospect?

There is no better way to learn more about the return of Jesus than in the context of God's overall plan for his world.

Dr. John Ecob has produced an amazing book titled *Eternity to Eternity*. It is written in a reader-friendly style and showcases many colourful charts and graphics to help you understand God's plan for the ages including, of course, the return of our Lord Jesus Christ.

- What were God's promises to Abraham? (Page 6)
- What happens beyond the grave? (Page 55)
- When will the Kingdom of Christ appear? (Page 57)
- The mystery church - will Jesus return for her? (Page 58)
- What is the first resurrection? (Page 60)
- Do you understand the book of Revelation? (Page 61)

A MUST-READ FOR EVERY SERIOUS CHRISTIAN

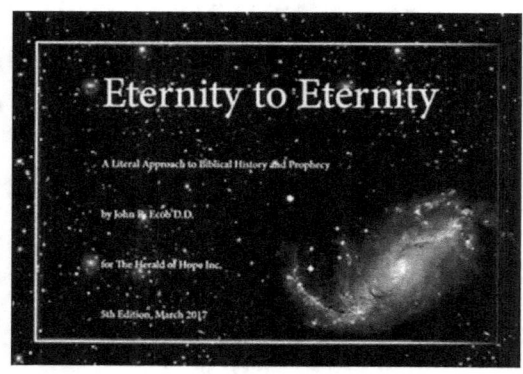

FREE DOWNLOAD FROM
www.biblicalpublications.org/ebooks.html

MARGARET'S TESTIMONY

A Testimony to the Grace of God

On a cold winter's evening in a small village in Europe, a little girl was born. Her parents loved her very much and had her christened into the Lutheran faith. They took her to church at Christmas and Easter, and in her mid-teens she attended Bible classes and was confirmed. But as she grew up, religious morals didn't suit her. After all, hadn't school taught her that the evolutionary process leaves all things to chance, and that everyone has the right to do as they please? So who was the church to make rules about right or wrong? She explained to her parents that science opposed the existence of absolute standards and decided to find her own way. Her name is Margaret – this is my life...

At age nineteen I met a young man from a far-away country and fell in love. We were married after two short months, and after another two years we left for his home in Australia. The Lutheran church and its ways had been completely discarded. Ten years passed and life was good. At age thirty-one, I had two small children, my husband owned a successful communication business, and I was practicing as a naturopath and clinical hypnotherapist. All was going to plan, but then something extraordinary happened. Two lovely ladies from New Tribes Mission came to see me as clients and, being curious, I asked them about their faith. I had turned to New Age concepts and joined the Rosicrucian Order, but I was always interested in the beliefs of others. One of the ladies (Jan) produced a little black Bible from her handbag and read the following verse: "For God so loved the world that he gave his only begotten Son, that whosoever believes in him should not perish but have everlasting life." I didn't object to a God of love, although I didn't really understand what that verse meant. But when she continued, saying that no one is righteous because all have sinned and fall short of the glory of God, I became less agreeable. "Stop right there," I responded, resisting this accusation. "I'm not a sinner! I'm not a liar or a thief or a murderer – to the contrary, I try to help people and am nice to them!" Jan was wise and did not argue. Instead, she read from Isaiah, chapter 53:6 that "all of us like sheep have gone astray; we have turned, every one, to his own way; and the LORD has laid on him (pointing to Jesus Christ) the iniquity (sin) of us all."

God used this portion of Scripture to cut right through me and convict me of sin. I felt so uncomfortable that I couldn't get rid of these women quickly enough. I tried to forget about the whole thing, but it didn't work. The thoughts about sin kept coming back to mind, and I soon grasped that sin was essentially SELF-WILL and therefore rebellion against God. The more I thought about it, the more I understood that I had a dilemma on my hands: if this God of the Bible was real, he would send me to hell. So I wondered how I could know whether he really existed. Finally, I asked him to show me, not knowing what to expect. I neither heard a voice nor did I have an ecstatic experience, but by the end of that evening I could no longer carry my burden. I fell on my knees and cried out to God, shedding tears of shame and tears of sorrow for causing him so much pain. But there were also tears of joy because I realised that I had been forgiven, my debt was paid, and I was set free to live a new life in God. This is how I was born again and became his child on March 28, 1983.

I had been so blind, but now I could see! And what I saw was a huge mission field, starting with my own family. I eagerly read the Bible, and the Lord took me to a study group where I learned about God's principles for family life. I decided to put his word to the test and exchanged my feminist ideas for the role of godly wife and mother. I learned to be (more) submissive, to give my husband his rightful place as head of the family, and to treat my children as gifts from God to be nurtured and treasured. This was HARD, but God was faithful and gracious: a year later my husband experienced the new birth, and we were both baptised in a Baptist church. Our children grew more and more excited about this powerful, loving God they were hearing so much about, and I reconsidered my approach to helping people and abandoned all New Age practices, retaining only what was compatible with the Bible.

As the years passed, my husband's business became too much for us and was sold through very unusual circumstances, which were clearly an answer to prayer. We home-schooled our children and moved to the country, where I continued my practice. The Lord took us through many painful experiences along the way, but despite these trials we can say with certainty that God is good! Our children have grown to be strong in him, have married in the faith, and are now involved in their own Christian endeavours.

I can certainly testify to the fact that Jesus Christ does all things well! My favourite Bible verse fits our situation perfectly:

"Trust in the Lord with all your heart and lean not unto your own understanding. In all your ways acknowledge Him, and He shall direct your paths." (Proverbs 3:5-6)

I pray that if you have not done so already, you, too, will turn to Jesus Christ and gain access to eternal life in the presence of TRUE LOVE - our glorious God and Savior. I look forward to meeting you there!

With Christian love,

Margaret

MARGARET'S MINISTRIES

www.DrLepke.com.au

www.BiblicalPublications.org

YOUR WAY TO ETERNAL LIFE

The God of the Bible has done something absolutely amazing because he loves you and wants you to live with him for all eternity. But before we tell you what he did to make this possible, and how you can receive his free gift, you need to understand the bad news of who you are without him: a sinner destined for hell. The sad fact is that you have sinned and are therefore guilty before this holy God who must judge sin.

The Bible puts it this way:

As it is written: "THERE IS NONE RIGHTEOUS, NO, NOT ONE...
THERE IS NO FEAR OF GOD BEFORE THEIR EYES...
For all have sinned and fall short of the glory of God."(Romans 3:10,18,23)
Jesus said: *And do not fear those who kill the body but cannot kill the soul. But rather fear Him (God) who is able to destroy both soul and body in hell. (Matthew 10:28)*

But God has a solution for the problem of your sin!

"For God so loved the world that He gave His only begotten Son, that whoever believes in Him should not perish but have everlasting life."

"He who believes in the Son has everlasting life; and he who does not believe the Son shall not see life, but the wrath of God abides on him."

The good news is...

You can escape God's judgement! He wants you to know that he loves you and that his Son died on the cross to pay the penalty for your sins. He wants you to know that Jesus rose from the dead and is now alive, ready and able to save you and give you everlasting life if you turn to him for forgiveness. Jesus has the power to transform your life! He has transformed ours, and he is waiting to do the same for you. Will you join us in serving this risen savior?